Map Symbols

POLITICAL BOUNDARIES

International
State and Provincial
County
Trusteeship Areas

CITIES, TOWNS AND VILLAGES

Principal Areas

Other cities, towns, and villages
are indicated by size of type and
symbol according to population.

County Seats are indicated by
dot-centered symbol.

Capital Cities

MISCELLANEOUS

National Parks
and Monuments

Railroads (Initialed in
U.S. and Canada)

NYC

Ruins
Dikes
Bridges
Dams
Canals

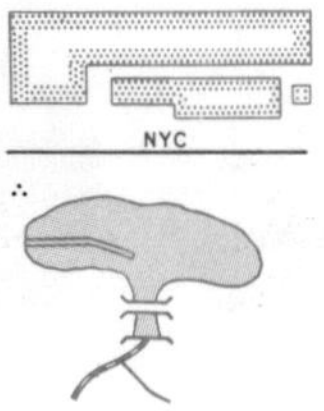

PHYSICAL FEATURES

Ranges →
Peaks →
Passes → SOUTH PASS
Point of Elevation
above level → 7,268 FT.
Escarpments, Bluffs
Cliffs and Plateaus
PLATEAU
Glaciers →
Volcanoes →
Lava Flows →
Sand Dunes →
Deserts →
Swamps and Marshes →

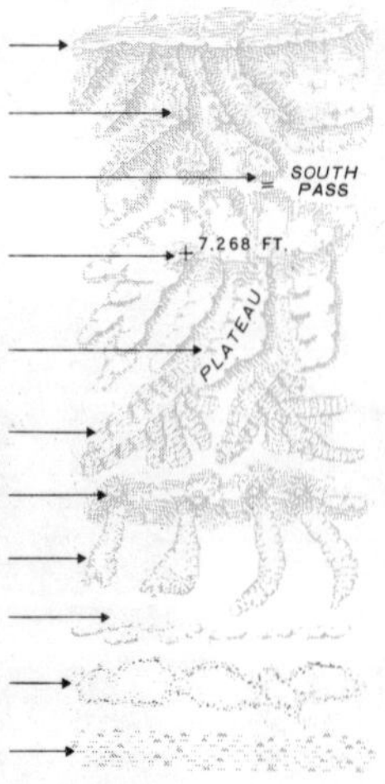

Countries in this Volume

Explanation of the Index Reference System in Volume 1, page 5.

RAND McNALLY
ILLUSTRATED ATLAS
OF TODAY'S WORLD

VOLUME
2

SOUTHERN AND EASTERN EUROPE
AND THE SOVIET UNION

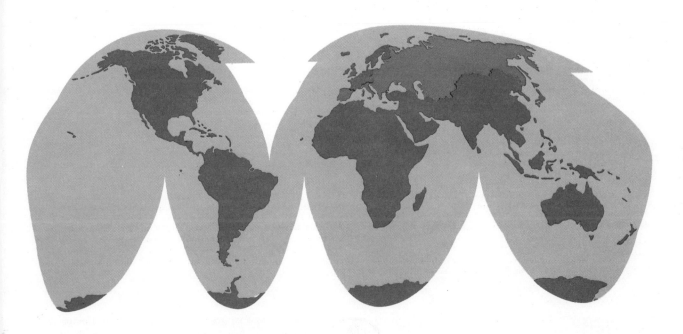

RAND McNALLY & COMPANY NEW YORK / CHICAGO / SAN FRANCISCO

ADVISORY BOARD

Fred W. Foster, Ph. D.
Professor of Geography
University of Illinois

Hans Morgenthau, Ph. D.
Professor of Political Science
and History
University of Chicago

J. Lewis Robinson, Ph. D.
Professor of Geography and
Chairman of the Department
University of British Columbia

STAFF

Editor-Text
Lewis W. Gillenson

Writers
Donald Allen
Stanley H. Brown
Caroline Byass
Eugene Dunlop
Darlene Geis
Peggy Lampl
David Landman
Frank Latham
Leonard Louis Levinson
Alan Littell
Hubert Pryor

Managing Editor
Dolores Field

Associate Editor
Helen Harter

Copy Editor
Ann Bishop

Cartography
The Cartographic
Staff of
Rand McNally
& Company

Art Director
Chris J. Arvetis

Designer
Gordon Hartshorne

Layout
Mario Pagliai
Terry Rose

Picture Editor
Alice P. Galway

Illustrations
Charles Moser

CREDITS

COVER: Harrison Forman; Foto Find (Jack Sterling); Shostal (2); Three Lions (2).
Panel, pages 94-95: Courtesy Sources—Canadian Pacific Railway; U. S. Air Force. Additional Sources—Alex O. Cox; Harrison Forman; Lanks from Monkmeyer; Shostal (Cutler J. Coulson, Steve Crouch, J. D. Winbray); Ed Snyder; Three Lions.
96 (top), Kerwin B. Roche; 96 (bottom), Peter Throckmorton from Nancy Palmer Agency; 97, J. Allan Cash from Rapho-Guillumette; 102, Louis Goldman from Rapho-Guillumette; 103 (top), J. Allan Cash from Rapho-Guillumette; 103 (bottom), Sabine Weiss from Rapho-Guillumette; 106, Ormond Gigli from Rapho-Guillumette; 110, George Pickow from Three Lions; 111, Dave Forbert from Shostal; 112, William H. Greene from Photo Researchers; 113, Tom Hollyman from Photo Researchers; 114, Ned Haines from Rapho-Guillumette; 116, Ace Williams from Photo Researchers; 117, Courtesy of Italian State Tourist Office; 120, Louis Renault from Photo Researchers; 121, David Seymour from Magnum; 123, Leonard von Matt from Rapho-Guillumette; 125, Chris Arvetis; 128, Philip Gendreau; 129, Henri Cartier-Bresson from Magnum; 130, Vasso Ningos from Globe Photos; 132 (top), Norman Pounds from Paul Popper, Ltd.; 132 (bottom), Harrison Forman from Shostal; 133 and 136, Marilyn Silverstone from Nancy Palmer Agency; 140, F.P.G.; 141, J. L. Stage from Photo Researchers; 143, Sid Feder from F.P.G.; 145, Alfred Von Sprary from Black Star; 146, Eastfoto; 148; Jerry Cooke from Photo Researchers; 152, Louis Renault from Photo Researchers; 153, Thomas Hopker from Rapho-Guillumette; 154, Joseph Tuszewski from PIX; 155, Shostal; 157, Claude Jacoby from PIX; 158, F.P.G.; 159, Marilyn Silverstone from Nancy Palmer Agency; 164, F.P.G.; 167, Eddy Posthuma de Boer from Black Star; 172 (top), Jerry Cooke from Photo Researchers; 172 (bottom), Harrison Forman; 174, Robert C. Lautman from F.P.G.; 175 (top left), George Holton from Photo Researchers; 175 (top right), M. Redkin from Sovfoto; 175 (bottom), Marilyn Silverstone from Nancy Palmer Agency; 176, Harrison Forman from Shostal; 178, Dana Brown from F.P.G.; 179, Jerry Cooke from Photo Researchers.

Contents

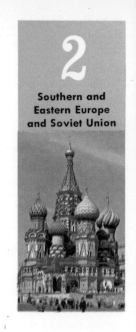

Introduction to

SOUTHERN AND EASTERN EUROPE
AND THE SOVIET UNION

The lands of Southern and Eastern Europe and the Soviet Union include territories of both the earliest super-power, the Roman Empire, and the newest, the Soviet Empire—the USSR and its Communist satellites. Although the Russians are Europeans, their nation has twice as much territory in Asia as in Europe. Between Portugal, the westernmost country of Southern Europe, and the easternmost point of the Soviet Union lies the entire span of Europe and Asia.

This vast territory comprises several distinct regions: the Atlantic coastal zone; the predominantly Mediterranean lands of Spain, Italy, Greece and Albania; the Balkan Peninsula between the Adriatic and the Black Sea including Yugoslavia, Bulgaria, and Romania; the Central European plains and mountains of Poland, Czechoslovakia, and Hungary; the European USSR, and, beyond the Urals, the lofty highlands, and the deserts, steppes, forests, and arctic tundras of Soviet Asia.

Near the Atlantic, the Mediterranean, and the Black Sea, the climate is mild, with adequate rain. But in the central plateau of Spain and from Central Europe eastward through the Soviet Union, continental climatic patterns prevail. This kind of climate is characterized by increasingly extreme summers and winters and dryness as one moves inland, away from the ocean. The Pacific region, on the other hand, has a climate with summer rain and dry winters.

The topography has all the variety to be expected in such a vast area. There are thousands of miles of coasts, towering mountains that form national boundaries and internal barriers, forests, meadows, and immense grasslands, arctic wastelands, and burning deserts. Great rivers and lakes water these lands, and numerous islands add to the territory.

Southern Europe has been the source of much that is great in western civilization, which stems directly from the scientific, artistic, and philosophical enlightenment of ancient Greece, and from the concepts of law and government and of language spread by Rome. Christianity became a great bond within the region.

With the temporary Arab conquests in the Iberian Peninsula (Spain and Portugal), and Sicily, and the advance in the Balkans of their successors, the Ottoman Turks, Moslem culture enriched this heritage. Then, some 600 years ago, the Renaissance, an excit-

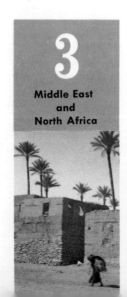

ing period of learning and culture, began in Italy and foundations of the scientific and industrial revolutions to come were laid.

In the Age of Exploration that followed the Renaissance, western civilization was carried around the world by the galleons of Spain and Portugal, and by the merchant ships of northern Europe.

The nations of Southern Europe had relatively few of the natural resources required for an industrial revolution. When it came to Western Europe and the New World, along with the invigorating power of the modern democratic governments, it scarcely touched Southern Europe. The economy of that area remained predominantly agricultural. The standard of living of the peasants was low. Government was not progressive. Only recently has this situation begun to change—especially in Italy.

The history of Eastern Europe followed a different course. Roman law and language were not carried much beyond the Danube River. Slavic tribes filled Eastern Europe after the original Germanic peoples left to overrun the Roman Empire. These immigrants lagged behind the southern Europeans in political, economic, and social development. They also were alien to them in speech and culture. The Slavs were the ancestors of the present-day peoples of Greater Russia, Poland, Czechoslovakia, Yugoslavia, and part of Romania. The Magyars invaded Hungary. Baltic tribes established themselves in Latvia and Lithuania. Germanic and Magyar minorities found homes in Romania. Turkic peoples spread into what is now Bulgaria, adopting Slavic speech. These peoples became Christians in the Middle Ages. Most Central Europeans were converted by the Roman Catholic Church; the Russians and most Balkan peoples were converted by Greek Orthodox missionaries from the Byzantine Empire, which began as the eastern branch of the Roman Empire.

Mongol invasions from Asia in the thirteenth century, Turkish conquests from the south in the four-teenth century, and continuing pressure from the Germanic nations of the west kept the region underdeveloped and in turmoil. Most of Central Europe and the Balkans did not regain full independence until the twentieth century.

The Russians are a special case. They threw off the Mongol yoke and by the eighteenth century had extended their domain to approximately its present size. This empire was transformed into a communist state by the revolution of 1917. Since then, by the forced mobilization of all aspects of national life, the Soviet Union has become a great industrial and agricultural producer. Perhaps more important, it has also become the political and ideological overlord of the other nations of Eastern Europe. These nations became communist after World War II.

The Soviet Union has, in quantity, supplies of almost every industrial raw material needed to make it self-sufficient. Compared with Southern Europe, the Soviet satellites also have considerable mineral wealth. Industry was well-developed in pre-Communist Poland and Czechoslovakia. Now these countries and the other eastern European nations are undergoing accelerated programs of industrialization under state control. Nevertheless, the region as a whole continues to rely on agriculture, also state controlled, for the greater part of its national income. Living standards, as in southern Europe, are low. Trade is almost entirely directed within the Communist bloc and with the underdeveloped countries of Asia and Africa, which the Communists are cultivating.

Thus, both Southern Europe and Eastern Europe are belatedly striving to catch up with the industrial West, though by different means. Southern Europe is working toward integration with the democratic European community. Eastern Europe, with its ties to Russia, is following the path of Communism. These political philosophies have divided Europe. As Winston Churchill said in 1946, "An Iron Curtain has descended across the continent."

7

United States I

8

United States II

9

Latin America

10

Australia, Oceania, and Polar Regions

11

Our World

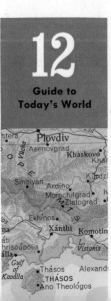

12

Guide to Today's World

In Rome, Italy, the ruins of the Forum still stand as a reminder of the glories of the ancient Empire. Here the Roman citizens met to transact business and discuss politics.

Beautiful natural harbors and picturesque villages line the sunny coasts of Greece. Fishing has long been a major Grecian occupation, and tourist resorts are of growing importance.

SOUTHERN EUROPE

The countries of Southern Europe owe much of their character to the Mediterranean Sea. The ancient Romans who once ruled the entire region called the Mediterranean *Mare Nostrum,* "our sea." It washes the shores of all major Southern Europe countries except Portgual. The countries are also blessed with the Mediterranean climate—hot, dry summers and cool, rainy winters. This climate prevails throughout the region except on the Atlantic coasts of Portugal and northern Spain, which are cooler and rainier, and in the high central plateau of Spain and the highland regions, where the winter is more severe.

Mountain barriers, such as the Pyrenees between Spain and France and the Alps ringing northern Italy cut off the Mediterranean lands from the rest of Europe. Other mountains, such as the Sierras that divide Spain and the rugged terrain of Albania and Greece, cut the peoples of Southern Europe off from their neighbors. The Mediterranean Sea, in contrast, has long been a highroad of cultural and commercial exchange. The ancient Greeks explored and colonized the Mediterranean coast. The Romans followed, consolidating their conquests until nearly the whole region knew the civilizing effect of Roman law and the unifying heritage of the Latin tongue.

The Mediterranean climate favors the crops common to all the countries of Southern Europe: cereal grains, olives, wine grapes, other fruits, nuts, vegetables, and, in a few districts, rice and tobacco. Sheep and goats are raised in the drier sections, while cattle are found wherever more plentiful rainfall keeps the pastures green. Much farming is done in the main river valleys, such as the Douro and Tagus in Portugal, the Ebro and Guadalquivir in Spain, and the Po in Italy.

Groves of olive trees in Toledo, Spain, which produces more olives than any other country in the world.

WESTERN MEDITERRANEAN
✪ Capitals

COSMO SERIES W. MEDITERRANEAN
Copyright by
RAND McNALLY & COMPANY
Made in U.S.A.

Lambert Conformal Conic Projection
SCALE 1 : 8,000,000   1 Inch = 126 Statute Miles

EASTERN MEDITERRANEAN

COSMO SERIES E. MEDITERRANEAN
A-55292/1
Copyright by
RAND McNALLY & COMPANY
Made in U.S.A.

Longitude East of Greenwich

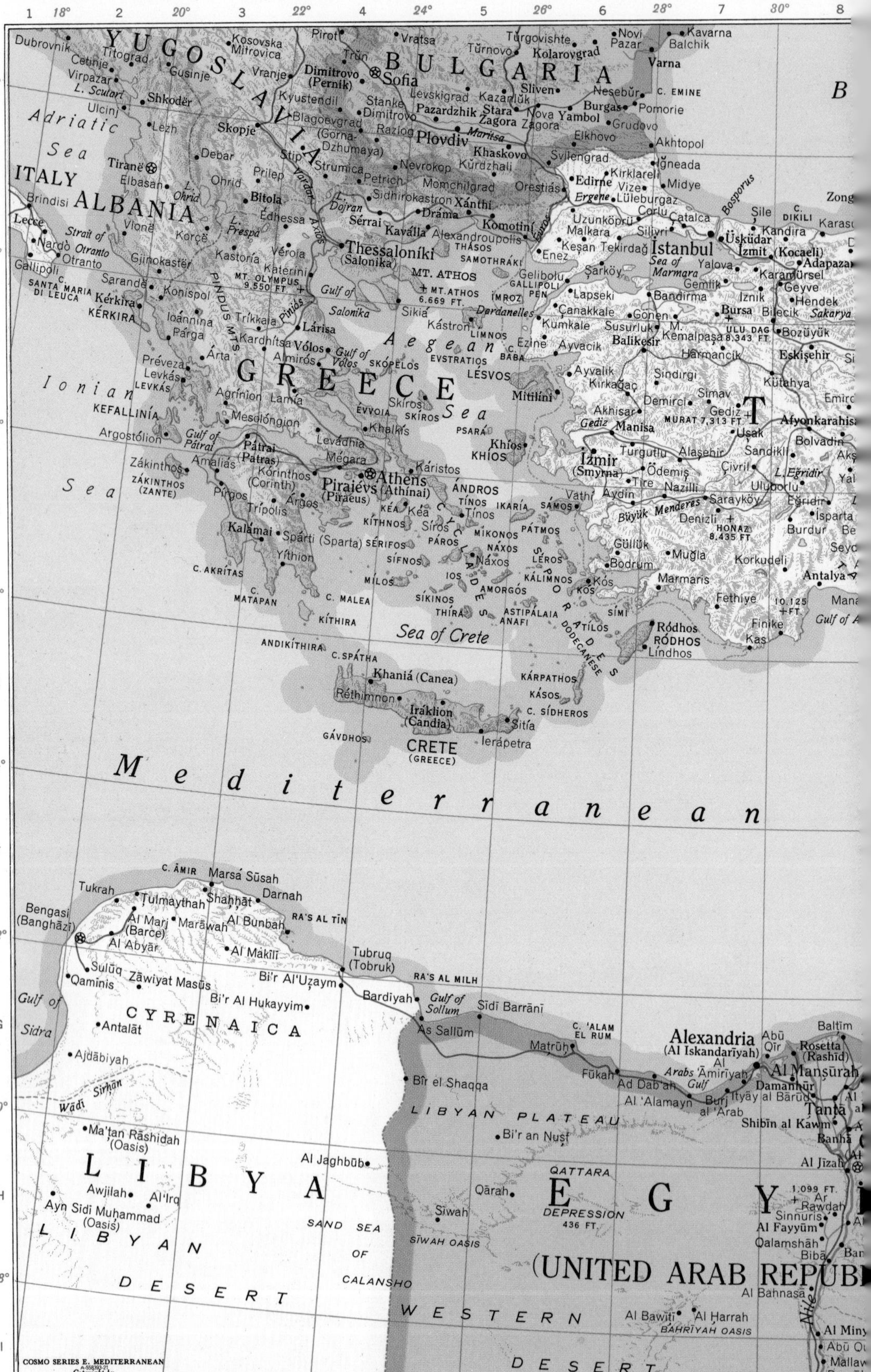

Statute Miles 50 0 50 100 150

Kilometers 50 0 50 100 200

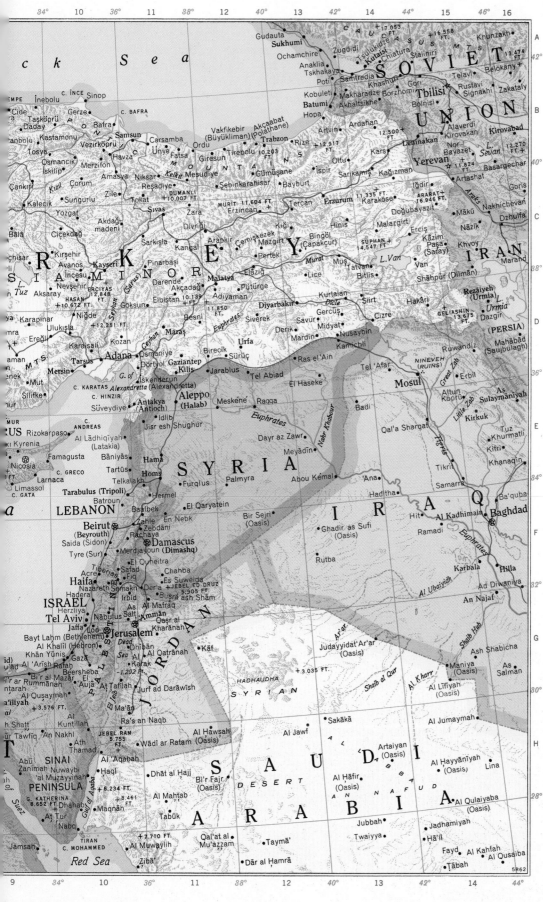

Lambert Conformal Conic Projection

SCALE 1:8,000,000 1 Inch = 126 Statute Miles

Most of the people of Southern Europe earn their living from farming or from food processing. By contrast with the farmers of Northern Europe their standard of living is low. The average per capita income for people of the southermost districts is less than $200 a year. In the richest area of the region, northern Italy with its many industries, the figure rises to about $500 a year.

Industry is not yet highly developed in most of Southern Europe. The region is not well supplied with mineral resources. Also, the Industrial Revolution was slow to reach these lands. Greece and Albania were long under the rule of the Turkish empire, and Italy was not united under one government until the 1870's. Today industry is growing, even in the most backward regions.

Portugal mines iron, coal, and tungsten. Albania has copper and some iron and petroleum. Greece produces the ore of aluminum, while Italy exploits deposits of mercury, sulfur, and oil. Only Spain, however, has truly significant mineral resources. Valuable deposits of coal and iron supply a steel industry, centered on Bilbao, and the factories of Barcelona. Mercury, copper, lead, and other ores are mined also.

Though Italy has few basic raw materials for industry, it makes up for the lack with skill. Industries centered in Milano (Milan) and Torino (Turin) turn out such highly diversified products as cars, office machines, electrical equipment, textiles, chemical products, and heavy machinery. Italy is the only country in Southern Europe with membership in the European Common Market. It is oriented toward collaboration with the major industrial powers.

Many waves of migration and conquest have swept

Mount Vesuvius, the only active volcano on the European mainland, towers over the Bay of Naples and the city, in southern Italy.

across Southern Europe. The people who live there today are the product of the mixing of many stocks, although each country has developed distinctive customs and language. However, political, ethnic, and linguistic boundaries do not always coincide. In the Iberian peninsula there are three political units—Spain, Portugal, and Andorra—but four languages. Portuguese is spoken in northwest Spain as well as in Portugal; Catalan is used in the east from Valencia to the Pyrenees and on into France; and Basque, a unique language, straddles the western end of the Pyrenees. Spanish is spoken in the rest of the peninsula.

Italians today are the product of innumerable blendings with the peoples of the eastern Mediterranean, North Africa, and with barbarians from Central Europe, as well as the original Italic tribes. So too with the Greeks, who have been infiltrated by Nordic, Slavic, and Turkish elements. The Albanians, with their clan system and curious language are believed to be descended from the Illyrian tribes who inhabited parts of Greece even before the Greeks arrived.

The Latin of Rome is the basis of the Portuguese, Spanish, and Italian tongues, while modern Greek is derived from ancient Greek, with some Turkish words. The Maltese dialect is compounded of Arabic and Italian. Albanian is an Indo-European tongue not closely related to either Greek or Latin.

The great capitals of Southern Europe have played a leading role in the development and spread of western civilization. Athens, the birthplace of democracy; Rome, the first "world capital" and long the center of Christendom; Madrid and Lisbon, the headquarters of empires that carried western ways around the world, are today modern seats of government. Albania, whose capital is Tiranë, is the only Communist nation in the region and today is isolated from the other countries.

The combination of pleasant climate, striking scenery, and varied peoples, along with the rich panorama of history and art to be found in Southern Europe, make tourism a major industry. Each year hundreds of thousands of visitors flock to its beaches, mountain resorts, and cities. They come to admire the Acropolis in Athens, cruise among the Greek islands, see the ruins of Rome by moonlight, or make a pilgrimage to St. Peter's, the great church in Vatican City. They visit the art galleries of Florence, drift in gondolas on the canals of Venice, breathe the pure air of the Italian lakes and Alps, or bake on the sands of the Costa Brava in Spain or Estoril in Portugal. They attend opera in Milan and Naples and bullfights in Sevilla. Such attractions as these make Southern Europe one of the most beautiful and fascinating regions of the earth.

An ornate twelfth-century Moorish tower in Seville, Spain.

These Portuguese women, carrying handmade brooms on their heads, are on their way to market to sell them.

MEDITERRANEAN LANDS: PHYSICAL APPEARANCE

The map represents land elevation by showing the landscape strongly lighted from the northwest. Highlights and shadows define the mountains and hills.

Longitude West of Greenwich 0° Longitude East of Greenwich

PORTUGAL

▲ SEE MAP PAGES 108–109

Capital: Lisbon

Population (1962): 9,000,000

Density: 247 per square mile
Distribution: Urban: 27 per cent
Rural: 73 per cent

Area: 36,376 square miles

Elevation: Highest point: 7,615 feet
(Azores Is.)
Lowest point: Sea level

Principal language: Portuguese

Principal religion: Catholicism

Political divisions: 22 districts

Currency unit: Escudo

National holiday: December 1, Independence
Day

National anthem: *A Portugesa*
(The Portuguese Girl)

Cork is Portugal's most valuable export.

Portugal's location, in the southwest corner of Europe, has exposed it to three distinct influences. One coastline faces west on the Atlantic Ocean, the other south toward Africa. Its back touches Spain.

The Atlantic Ocean brings warm breezes and adequate rainfall to many parts of the country during the winter months. Along its coasts are excellent sandy beaches and many seaside resorts.

The long coastline facing the Atlantic Ocean encouraged Portuguese exploration. Until the fifteenth

Nazare, a few miles north of Lisbon, is one of Portugal's principal fishing ports.

SCALE
75 Miles

PORTUGAL
ECONOMY

ECONOMY

HEAVY INDUSTRY

- Iron
- Machinery
- Steel
- Transportation Equipment

LIGHT INDUSTRY

- Chemicals
- Food Processing
- Leather Products
- Lumber & Forest Products
- Metal Products
- Pulp & Paper Products
- Stone Clay & Glass Products
- Textiles
- Cotton
- Linen
- Wineries Breweries Distilleries
- Jewelry

OTHERS

- Fishing
- Seaport
- Water Power
- Fishing Areas

MINING

- An Antimony
- C Coal
- Cu Copper
- Cr Chromite
- I Iron Ore
- L Lead
- Li Lignite
- Py Pyrites
- Sn Tin
- Tu Tungsten

© RMSN & CO.

AGRICULTURE

- Mediterranean Agriculture
- Forestry with some Farming and Pasture
- Non-Agricultural Areas
- Seasonal Grazing with Nomadic Herding
- Seasonal Grazing with Sparse Agriculture

sailed down the coast of Africa past the Cape of Good Hope in 1488. His was the first European ship to reach the southern tip of Africa.

In 1497, Vasco da Gama, another Portuguese captain, made the first sea trip from Europe to India. Ferdinand Magellan, whose fleet was the first to sail around the world, was also Portuguese, though he sailed in the service of Spain. These and other traders and explorers helped to make Portugal the center of a great empire, some of which still remains.

Portuguese explorations went far beyond Africa. In 1542, the Portuguese made the first European contact with Japan. They also began trade with the East Indies about that time. The territory of Macao, a peninsula and two islands on the China coast near Hong Kong, has been occupied by the Portuguese for centuries.

Mountains cut off most of Portugal from easy access to the more populous areas of Spain and to the rest of the European continent by land. But Portugal has had close ties via the sea with Great Britain for many years. The English gave help to Portugal in the seventeenth century, when the Portuguese were fighting one of their many wars with Spain, a traditional rival of Britain for control of the seas. Later, British investors financed many miles of railroad and city transportation lines in Lisbon, the capital. Today, British families and companies own large farm estates and industries in Portugal. England is the principal customer for port wine, one of Portugal's most important export products.

Plentiful rainfall in the southern plains area encourages the growth of thick forests, mostly of cork oak trees. The stripped cork bark is Portugal's leading export, followed by sardines. Fish from the Atlantic waters also provide the Portuguese with their most important domestic food product, *bacalhau*, dry, salted codfish that is eaten daily in much of the country. The skilled Portuguese fishermen are famous far beyond Portugal. Their fishing fleets roam the world's oceans. Portuguese fishermen have emigrated to other countries, too. There are numerous Portuguese communities along the Atlantic coast of the United States, especially in New England, where many engage in their traditional occupation.

More than half the people of Portugal work at farming. The chief products are olives, wine grapes, cereals, hogs, and sheep. Since the land in much of the country is not very fertile, the people must work hard to raise their crops and livestock. Some portions of the coastal plains are hot and dry, and grow little besides cactus. In the mountains, however, snow remains on the ground as late as April and begins falling again in December.

century, few ships ventured beyond the Mediterranean. During this century, Portuguese sea captains explored the Atlantic coast of Africa all the way to the Cape of Good Hope. Their efforts were inspired by a remarkable man known to history as Henry the Navigator, a younger son of the King of Portugal, who made the discovery of a way around Africa his life work. He himself did not sail on the expeditions. He was called "the Navigator" because of his contributions to the science of navigation. On the coast of Portugal, he established a school for sea captains. There he collected books, maps, and the best navigational instruments of his day. In this school Prince Henry trained the captains who went forth year after year, each year a little farther south along the coast of Africa. Bartholomew Diaz, a Portuguese captain,

SPAIN AND PORTUGAL

SPAIN
Principal Cities
Pop.—Thousands

77	Albacete	C 5
20	Alcalá	D 3
25	Alcázar de San Juan	C 4
25	Alcira	C 5
42	Alcoy	C 5
43	Algeciras	D 3
109	Alicante	C 5
21	Almendralejo	C 2
67	Almería	D 4
22	Andújar	C 3
30	Antequera	D 3
22	Aranjuez	B 4
21	Ávila	B 3
59	Badajoz	C 2
60	Badalona	B 7
41	Baracaldo	A 4
1,429	Barcelona	B 7
255	Bilbao	A 4
62	Burgos	A 4
50	Cáceres	C 2
109	Cádiz	D 2
27	Carmona	D 3
69	Cartagena	D 5
58	Castellón de la Plana	C 5
21	Cieza	C 5
33	Ciudad Real	C 4
182	Córdoba	D 3
24	Cuenca	B 4
20	Daimiel	C 4
23	Don Benito	C 3
30	Écija	D 3
20	Elda	C 5
35	Elche	C 5
47	El Ferrol [del Caudillo]	A 1
28	El Puerto de Santa María	D 2
26	Gerona	B 7
111	Gijón	A 3
154	Granada	D 4
19	Guadalajara	B 4
23	Guadix	D 4
19	Guecho	A 4
70	Hospitalet	B 7
63	Huelva	D 2
20	Huesca	A 5
19	Irún	A 5
67	Jaén	D 4
79	Jerez de la Frontera	D 2
157	La Coruña	A 1
55	La Línea	D 3
72	León	A 3
62	Lérida	B 6
44	Linares	C 4
21	Lorca	D 5
25	Lucena	D 3
62	Lugo	A 2
1,849	Madrid	B 4, p17
304	Málaga	D 3
19	Manacor	C 7
40	Manresa	B 6
18	Manzanares	C 4
22	Martos	D 4
31	Mataró	B 7
22	Mérida	C 2
20	Montilla	D 3
22	Morón de la Frontera	D 3
19	Motril	D 4
57	Murcia	D 5
72	Orense	A 2
20	Osuna	D 3
88	Oviedo	A 3
154	Palma [de Mallorca]	C 7
68	Pamplona	A 5
28	Peñarroya-Pueblonuevo	C 3

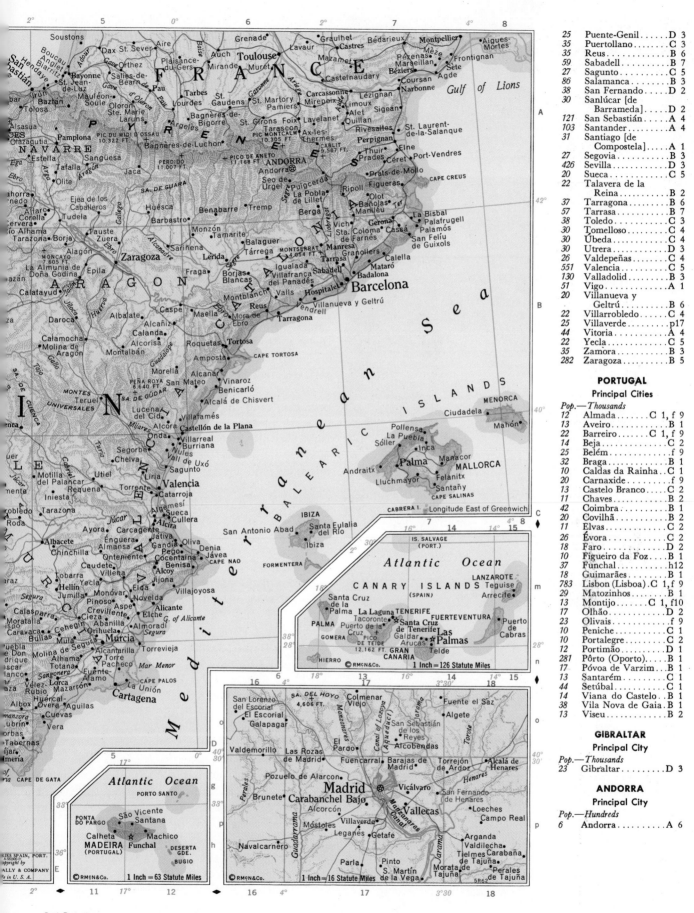

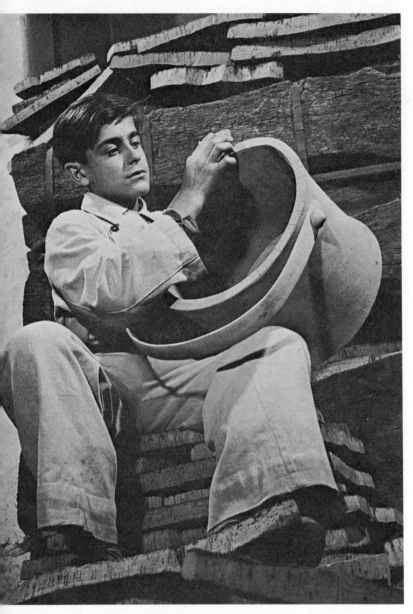

A Portuguese craftsman makes a bucket of cork. Cork, the bark of the cork oak tree, is a valuable product of Portugal.

Traces of the history of the country are apparent in the Chinese and Moorish influences in architecture and design. Many buildings have curved pagoda-style roofs that point back to the time when Portugal became the first European nation to trade with China. The intricate designs painted on the colorful tile used on many of the buildings reflect the strong influence of the Moslem Moors of North Africa. They invaded the country in the eighth century and remained until 1249. In that year, they were finally driven out of the Algarve (Ahl-*ghar*-vi), the southernmost province of Portugal.

The Moorish influence was deeply stamped into the Portuguese way of life. Though the Portuguese language is derived from Latin, as is Spanish, it also contains many Arabic words. The presence of the Moors may also be seen in the physical characteristics of many of the people. The Portuguese have generally been free of racial prejudice, and wherever they have settled, they have mixed and married.

Portugal remained an independent nation from the time of the defeat of the Moors until 1580. In that year, the Spanish claimed and took the Portuguese throne. The Spanish rulers were ousted in 1640. From then on, the Portuguese ruled themselves, except for a period after 1807, when Napoleon invaded the country. The ruling family moved to Brazil, then a Portuguese colony, and remained there until 1820.

Portugal's last king was Manuel II, who was ousted in 1910, when Portugal became a republic. The new government failed to prevent a series of economic and political crises. As a result, in 1932, Antonio Salazar came to power as prime minister, and then became dictator. He had been a professor of economics at the University of Coimbra (Koh-*em*-bra) and had also served as finance minister.

His administration at first brought the nation some economic and industrial progress. But it crushed opposition, denied civil liberties, and eventually diminished creative incentive. Too little has been done to advance the low educational level of the people. The illiteracy rate of Portugal remains one of the highest in Europe. Only about 60 per cent of the Portuguese people can read. Yet Portugal's University of Coimbra, founded in the thirteenth century, was one of the first in Europe.

Portugal's once vast colonial empire has shrunk considerably. The Dutch captured the East Indies centuries ago, and the empire lost another major part in 1822, when Brazil declared its independence. In 1962, India took the colony of Goa and two other small areas on the coast of India. The cities of Goa had been trading centers, under Portuguese rule, for more than 400 years.

The Azores and the Madeira Islands are "part" of Portugal (*see* Volume 3). The Azores lie about 1,000 miles west of Portugal in the Atlantic. They are very fertile and also are well located as a mid-Atlantic air base. Madeira lies southwest of Portugal off the Moroccan coast. It is famous for Madeira wine. Portugal also has owned colonies on both the east and west coasts of Africa. Bitter nationalistic independence movements, especially in Angola on the west coast, have cost Portugal heavily in military defences. If the European colonies will eventually be freed, Portugal will face the new problem of adjusting to the loss of its overseas resources.

SPAIN

▲ SEE MAP PAGES 108–109

Capital: Madrid

Population (1962): 30,525,000
    Density: 157 per square mile
    Distribution: Urban: 34 per cent
             Rural: 66 per cent

Area: 194,345 square miles

Elevation: Highest point:
    12,198 feet (Canary Islands);
    11,168 feet (Continental Spain)
    Lowest point: Sea level

Principal language: Spanish

Principal religion: Roman Catholicism

Political divisions: 50 provinces

Currency unit: Peseta

National holiday: May 2, Dos de Mayo
    (Beginning of the War
    of Independence against
    France, 1808)

National anthem: *Marcha de los Grenade-*
    ros (The Grenadiers)

A fine-vintage sherry wine.

Within the past four hundred years, Spain prospered until it became the richest nation in Europe, and then it fell, and became one of the poorest. Spain grew wealthy as a result of explorations and conquests in the New World, beginning, of course, with Christopher Columbus' voyage in 1492. Spanish gold came from Cortés' Mexico, from Pizarro's Peru, and elsewhere in the vast new empire. At the beginning of the eighteenth century, Spain owned the Philippines, the Netherlands, part of Italy, and all of Central and South America, except Brazil.

In those days, the riches flowed in so copiously from the outside that the rulers of Spain did not trouble themselves to make their homeland productive. But, in the eighteenth and nineteenth centuries, war losses and successful independence movements in Latin America cost them much of their empire. They were forced to turn their attention to their home, a country with little fertile soil.

Most of Spain is made up of mountain ranges and high plateaus. Mountains extend across almost the entire northern edge of Spain and much of its southern coast. Chains of mountains also rise in Spain's interior between the plateaus. The best farmland is in the area around Valencia, which gave its name to a famous variety of orange. Big estates in Andalusia, in the southwest, produce large crops of wheat, olives, and

fruit, as well as herds of cattle. Almost half of Spain's total surface is devoted to farming and pasture, but most of it is not very productive.

Though the climate of Spain ranges from mild to hot in the summer, there is little rainfall in many areas even during the winter, which is called the rainy season. In some parts of the country, the farmers divert water from rivers and streams to irrigate their fields. On many of these irrigated farms, two crops a year are normal. Elsewhere one crop is the rule.

Lack of water has been the principal cause of the low productivity of Spanish agriculture. Recently the government has been irrigating undeveloped lands and settling farmers on them, but the farm problem remains a serious one. There are shortages of fertilizer

Lobster fishermen of northern Spain repair their gear. The basket-like traps are lowered to the bottom in shallow water.

SPAIN
ECONOMY

AGRICULTURE

	General Farming
	Pastureland & Fodder Crops
	Mediterranean Agriculture
	Seasonal Grazing, with Sparse Agriculture
	Forestry with some Farming and Pasture
	Seasonal Grazing with Nomadic Herding
	Forest & Wood Products
	Non-Agricultural Areas

SCALE
100 Miles

© R.M&N. & CO.

ECONOMY

HEAVY INDUSTRY

	Machinery		Transportation
	Iron		Equipment
St	Steel		

LIGHT INDUSTRY

	Electrical & Electronic Products		Stone Clay & Glass Products
	Chemicals		Textiles
	Clothing	C	Cotton
	Food Processing	S	Silk
	Furniture	W	Wool
	Leather Products		Tobacco Products
	Metal Products		Wineries Breweries Distilleries
	Printing & Publishing		Precision Tools & Equipment
	Pulp & Paper Products		

OTHERS

	Tourists & Resorts		Fishing
	Seaport		Fishing Areas

MINING

A	Asphalt	L	Lead	S	Silver
C	Coal	Li	Lignite	Sn	Tin
Cu	Copper	Mn	Manganese	T	Titanium
G	Gold	Mr	Mercury	Tu	Tungsten
I	Iron Ore	Pm	Petroleum	Z	Zinc

Sails unfurl in the wind on an old windmill near Cartagena, on the southeastern coast of Spain.

and draft animals. Money is needed to finance agricultural development, and scientific knowledge is needed to make the development successful.

Olives are grown on more land in Spain than any other crop except wheat. Olive trees are able to send their roots deep into the soil for water. The olives are usually pressed to extract oil, a basic source of fat in southern Europe. Another common crop is grapes, mostly used to make wine. Corn, beans, or potatoes are usually grown on the small farms for home use.

Spanish farms produce enough olive oil, wine, and oranges for export. But the Spanish must import some goods. Even though Spain is a maritime nation with a long coastline, fish must be imported from Portugal and elsewhere to supply domestic requirements.

Sheep raising is another major agricultural activity in Spain. Its principal product is wool, with sheep milk, cheese, and, to a lesser extent, meat as by-products. In recent years attempts have been made to limit grazing, because it has destroyed new grass crops and hastened soil erosion. New rail lines for shipping sheep from summer to winter pastures have decreased the damage caused by the herds as they graze along the routes.

Spain's towns and cities harbor a third of the nation's population. The country has many medium and large cities, some of which are important to the economy today. Others trace their importance to the past. On the northeast coast is Barcelona, Spain's second largest city with more than 1,500,000 people. Barcelona is the largest port and the major textile-manufacturing center of Spain. Bilbao (Bil-*bah*-o), on the north Atlantic coast, is another important industrial city, with the nation's largest steel mills. The steel industry of Bilbao uses ore mined in the nearby Cantabrian Mountains. Another metropolis of the north, Saragossa (Zaragoza, Thar-rah-*go*-tha), was named for the Roman emperor Augustus Caesar. In modern times, the city has become an important transportation center and a leader in sugar refining, flour milling, and food canning. Burgos, also in the north, is most famous as the birthplace of El Cid, Spain's national hero of the eleventh century. Burgos is also noted for its Gothic architecture.

Aside from Madrid, the capital, the most important city of the central belt of Spain is Valencia, on the Mediterranean. With a population exceeding a half-million, it is the third largest Spanish city. It is a major seaport, especially for shipping oranges, lemons, raisins, and wine. Its chief industries are silk manufacturing and chemical production.

Seville (Sevilla, Say-*vee*-lya) is the largest city of the south. Though located inland, it is a seaport because ocean-going vessels can reach it by a deep canal

At Jerez de la Frontera, the Marques de Torresoto is tasting his sherry wines. The word "sherry" is derived from the town name.

and river system. Seville once controlled the trade with all Spanish colonies. Before that, it was an important Moorish city during the time when the Moslem invaders occupied Spain. Many of Seville's buildings date from Moorish days, especially the famed Alcázar. Now Seville is an important industrial city.

Other important southern cities include the seaport and wine-producing center of Málaga (*Ma*-la-ga), Cádiz (*Kah*-diz), and the former Moorish capitals of Córdoba (*Kor*-du-vuh) and Granada.

Contrary to popular conception, the "typical" Spaniard does not really exist. The very dark gypsies of southern Spain are no more typical than the blond Catalans around Barcelona. The Catalan language is not even Spanish. It is related to Provençal, the dialect of southern France. In the northwest, the Galicians speak a dialect that is more like Portuguese than it is like Spanish.

The Basques, who live along the north coast of Spain and also across the border, in France, are Spain's most distinctive group. No one knows where they came from. Even their language is a puzzle; it is like no other in the world. Some authorities believe the Basques are descendants of the original settlers of the area. They are considered to be the best shepherds in Europe and are much in demand in the United States and other sheep-producing countries. The Basque national sport, *jai alai*, is one of the fastest and most difficult games in the world. It is also played in Florida, in Cuba, and elsewhere in Latin America, where it is usually called *pelota*. The Basques are a rugged, independent people, who have resisted almost every attempt of the Spanish to dominate them.

Spanish ore deposits were coveted by invaders as far back as early recorded history. The peninsula was taken by the ancient Phoenicians and then by the Greeks. Later it became a part of the Roman Empire. The same tribes that attacked and conquered Rome also invaded and settled in the Iberian Peninsula. They became Christians and formed several small kingdoms. In the eighth century, most of the peninsula fell to another wave of invaders, the Moslems from Arabia and North Africa. The Moors, as they were called in Spain, remained for almost 800 years. Although they had a great influence on the laws, language, learning, population, and architecture of Spain, they never succeeded in converting the people from

A bullfight in Seville, in southern Spain. Bullfighting is very popular and is considered to be the country's national sport.

Christianity to Islam, the religion of Mohammed.

After initial defeats, the Christian kingdoms gradually began to drive the Moors south over the peninsula. Finally, in 1492, Granada, the last Moorish stronghold, fell. The kingdoms of Spain were joined together under Ferdinand and Isabella, the rulers of Aragon and Castile. In that same year, Queen Isabella sent Christopher Columbus to find the Spice Islands.

From that beginning, Spain's colonial possessions increased. During the same period, the various kingdoms of Spain were merged into a single, all-powerful kingdom. Philip II, who ascended the throne in 1556, was the first absolute ruler of a united Spanish kingdom. Though his Armada was defeated by the English in 1588, Spain remained powerful for many years. As a leading champion of the Roman Catholic church in Europe, Spain fought in the continent's religious wars during the seventeenth century. Spain also fought in nearly all the European political wars of the eighteenth century, often to decide which member of what royal family would succeed to the throne of a nation. Spain gained territory in some of these wars, but its strength was also being drained.

In the beginning of the nineteenth century, Napoleon Bonaparte led his French armies into Spain and put his brother Joseph on the Spanish throne. Spain was the first European nation won back from Napoleon by the armies of the English Duke of Wellington.

During this early part of the nineteenth century, revolutions in Latin America led by Simon Bolívar, San Martín, Hidalgo, and other local leaders overthrew Spanish rule. By 1825, Spain had lost practically all of its former territories in the New World. In 1898, Spain suffered a quick, severe defeat by the United States in the Spanish-American War. It cost Spain Cuba, Puerto Rico, and the Philippines.

In 1931, the Spanish finally deposed their last king and established a republic. Five years later, a violent and bloody civil war broke out. It ended in March, 1939, with a victory for the insurgent forces of General Francisco Franco, who remained as dictator of Spain. The war cost the nation a million dead and exiled, and there was severe devastation from which Spain has still to recover fully.

Spain has given much to the world. Miguel de Cervantes was the author of *Don Quixote*, one of the great books of the world. El Greco, Velasquez, Goya, Dali, and Picasso are some of Spain's many outstanding painters. Spanish flamenco and bolero music is played everywhere. Spain gave its language and architectural style to nearly all of Central and South America, to the Philippines, and even to parts of Texas, New Mexico, and California.

ANDORRA

▲ SEE MAP PAGES 108–109

Capital: Andorra

Population (1962) 9,000

    Density: 51 per square mile

Area: 175 square miles

Elevation: Highest Point: 9,665 feet

    Lowest Point: 2,804 feet

Principal language: Catalan

Principal religion: Catholicism

Political divisions: 6 parishes

Currency unit: Peseta

National holiday: September 8

National anthem: *Himne Andorra* (The opening line, translated, reads: "The great Charlemagne, my Father")

A sure-footed Andorran mule.

This beautiful and inaccessible tiny state rests deep in the highlands of the Pyrenees, surrounded by mountain crests and cut by valleys that climb to impenetrable walls. Although it is a co-principality administered by both France and Spain since 1278, Andorra is traditionally independent, a historic proof of the proverb that to have two masters is to have none. Only the heads of families may vote, and they elect the twenty-four member governing body that deals with civil affairs. Its people are hardy mountain peasants who speak Catalan, a language of Latin derivation common to the people of the eastern Pyrenees.

Sheep breeding, tobacco raising and processing, and smuggling were, for many years, the foundation of Andorra's economy. In recent years, these sources of income have been generously supplemented by the revenues from two radio transmitters and from the increasing number of summer visitors.

GIBRALTAR

▲ SEE MAP PAGES 108–109

Capital: Gibraltar

Population (1962): 26,000

    Density: 13,000 per square mile

    Distribution: Urban: 100 per cent

        Rural: None

Area: 2 square miles

Elevation: Highest Point: 1,398 feet

    Lowest Point: Sea level

Principal languages: Spanish; English

Principal religions: Catholicism; Protestantism

Currency unit: Pound

Historically, control of the Straits of Gibraltar, the narrow body of water between Spain and North Africa, has meant control of the Mediterranean. Britain captured the peninsula, a narrow spit of land rising from low ground at the Spanish border to the towering Rock in the south, from Spain in the early 1700's and made it into a fortress. It is now a crown colony of the British Empire. The Rock is the home of the Barbary Apes. Gibraltar has a British naval and air base, and a deep harbor at the foot of the Rock.

ITALY

▲ SEE MAP PAGES 118–119

Capital: Rome

Population (1962): 49,700,000

Density: 427 per square mile

Distribution: Urban: 35 per cent

Rural: 65 per cent

Area: 116,303 square miles

Elevation: Highest point: 15,200 feet

Lowest point: Sea level

Principal language: Italian

Principal religion: Roman Catholicism

Political divisions: 19 regions, divided into 91 provinces

Currency unit: Lira

National holiday: June 2, Constitution Day

National anthem: *Inno de Mameli* (Mameli Hymn)

A typewriter, product of the highly skilled industry of northern Italy.

In northern Italy, a farm family spreads its corn crop to dry. At harvest time, everyone helps with the farm work.

Though only slightly larger in area than Arizona, Italy has geographic, language, and population differences enough for at least three separate nations. The people range in appearance from the dark-eyed, dark-skinned natives of Sicily and the peninsula south of Rome, to the blond, blue-eyed people in Tuscany and other more northern sections of the country.

The peninsular shape of Italy has been compared to a boot. The top of the boot fits snugly into the Alps, the heart of Europe. The toe points to Sicily, an island in the Mediterranean Sea. While a resort town in the northern Italian Alps was the scene of the 1956 Winter Olympic Games, many parts of the southern Italian mainland and Sicily are warm and sunny all winter, and frost is rare.

Melting snows from the Alps flood the Po River every spring. The Po rises in the mountains near the French border in the northwest, flows past the industrial city of Turin (Torino, To-*ree*-no), and empties into the Adriatic Sea south of Venice (Venezia, Ve-*nayt*-zee-ah). The Po Valley has the most fertile and productive farmland in Italy. It covers only about 15 per cent of the country, but its fields yield 60 per cent of the corn, 40 per cent of the wheat, most of the sugar beets, rice, cattle, hogs and other important food crops. While nearly two-thirds of the Italians live on farms, few farmers outside the Po Valley raise more food than they need for their own families.

Aside from the fertile Po Valley, most of the Italian peninsula is covered by steep hills and mountains. The mountains begin in France, cross the border on the shore of the Ligurian Sea, and extend south along the peninsula, west into the toe, and continue in Sicily. The island of Sardinia also is covered with rough hills and low mountains.

Although there are woodlands on some mountain sides, much of Italy's surface is bare and sun-baked. During the heavy winter and early spring rains, the ditches, streams, and rivers run yellow with the

ITALY
ECONOMY

ECONOMY

HEAVY INDUSTRY

- Machinery
- Metal Processing Iron
- Metal Processing Steel
- Metal Processing Aluminum
- Petroleum Refining
- Transportation Equipment Aircraft
- Transportation Equipment Automobiles
- Transportation Equipment Railroad
- Transportation Equipment Ship

LIGHT INDUSTRY

- Electrical & Electronic Products
- Chemicals
- Food Processing
- Furniture
- Leather Products
- Lumber & Forest Products
- Metal Products
- Printing & Publishing
- Pulp & Paper Products
- Motion Pictures
- Stone Clay & Glass Products
- Textiles
- Cotton
- Silk
- Textiles & Clothing
- Wineries Breweries Distilleries

OTHERS

- Fishing
- Seaport
- Tourists & Resorts
- Water Power
- Insurance
- Fishing Areas

MINING

- B Bauxite
- C Coal
- Cu Copper
- I Iron Ore
- L Lead
- Mr Mercury
- Mo Molybdenum
- Z Zinc
- Gs Natural Gas
- N Nickel
- Pm Petroleum
- Sa Salt
- Su Sulphur

AGRICULTURE

- Intensive Agriculture
- Mediterranean Agriculture
- General Farming
- Pastureland & Fodder Crops
- Seasonal Grazing, with Sparse Agriculture
- Forestry with some Farming and Pasture
- Non-Agricultural Areas

© RM&N & CO.

washed-off topsoil. When the rains cease, these same waterways all but dry up. In many dry areas, the only plants that can be grown profitably are olive trees and grapevines.

The major cities of Italy contrast sharply with the poverty of much of the countryside. They combine relics of Italy's great past with concrete, steel, and glass buildings that are among the most modern in the world. In Rome, ancient ruins stand side by side with new residential and commercial buildings. A modern apartment house at the edge of the Roman Forum includes part of the ancient structure in its foundation and remains of a medieval castle in its lower floors.

In general, northern Italy is more prosperous than southern Italy. In addition to the rich agricultural country of the Po Valley, the north also has most of Italy's industry. The area roughly bounded by the three cities of Genoa (Genova, *Je*-no-vah), Turin, and Milan is the industrial heart of Italy.

Italian factory workers are assembling motor scooters, an inexpensive and popular means of transportation.

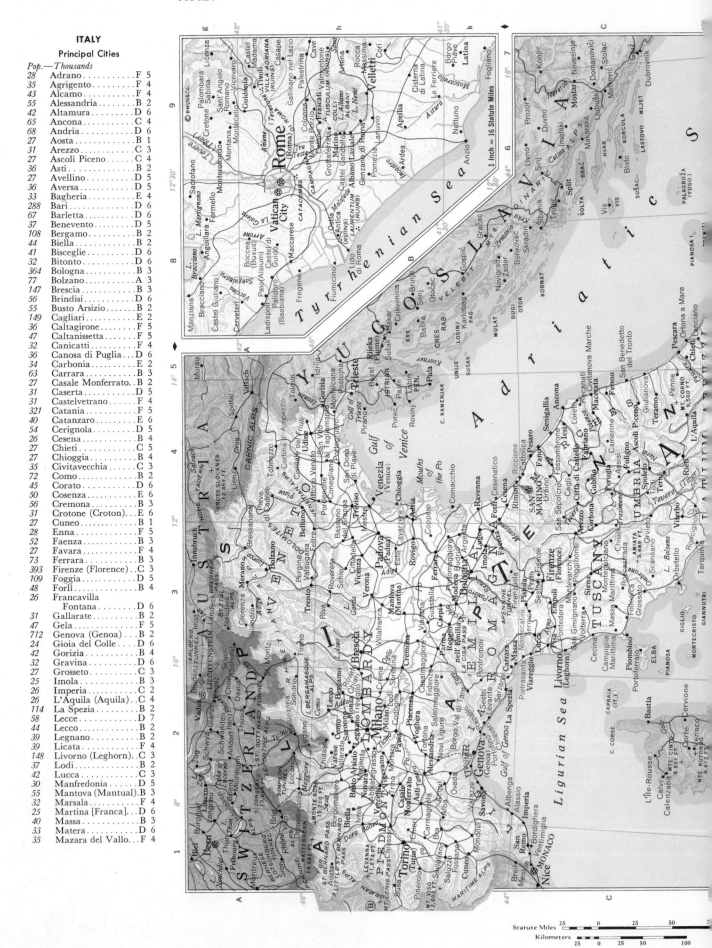

ITALY
Principal Cities
Pop.—Thousands

Statute Miles
Kilometers

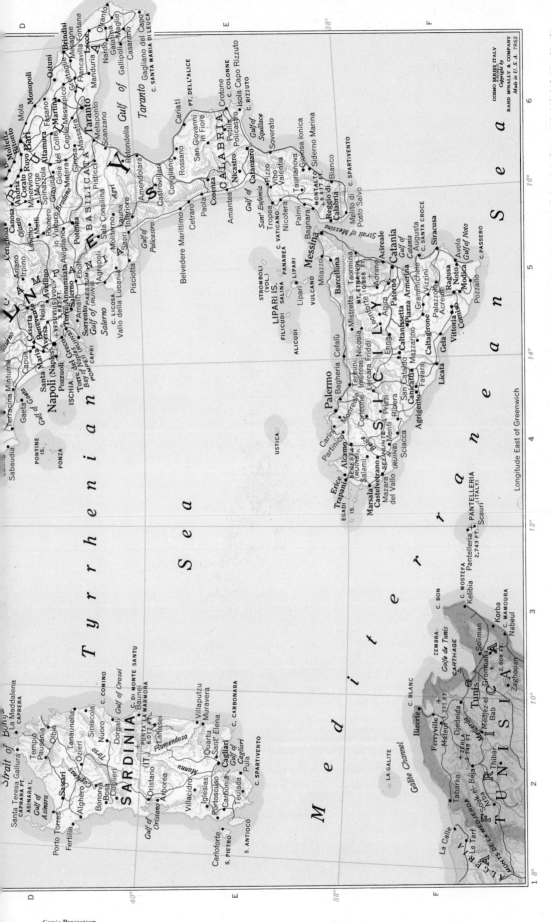

COSMO SERIES ITALY
Copyright by
RAND McNALLY & COMPANY
Made in U.S.A. 7R62

Conic Projection
SCALE 1:4,000,000 1 Inch = 63 Statute Miles

SAN MARINO

Principal City

Pop.—Thousands

VATICAN CITY

Principal City

Pop.—Hundreds

Eternal Rome, Italy's capital, is a city of imposing buildings, magnificent avenues, and haunting beauty.

The great northern city, Milan (Milano, Mi-*lahn*-oh), is Italy's commercial and financial capital, the location of the principal Italian stock exchange.

The modern factories around Turin produce automobiles, locomotives, machine tools, and other durable goods, silks and textiles. Since World War II, Italy has become a major producer of steel and chemicals. Hydroelectric plants in the Po River Valley provide much of the power for this industry. Italy is said to be Europe's largest producer of hydro power.

The city of Florence (Firenze, Fee-*ren*-tse), in the province of Tuscany, contrasts sharply with Milan. Though it has some modern buildings and facilities, it is principally a museum of past greatness. There are important Roman ruins near Florence. But its main importance rests with its many art and architecture treasures from the Renaissance, the period of rebirth of art and learning in the fourteenth, fifteenth, and sixteenth centuries.

Naples (Napoli, *Na*-po-lee), located in the south, on the Gulf of Naples, is another of the great cities of Italy. The word "Neapolitan" often brings to mind happy songs, street dances, and balmy nights. In re-

cent years, Naples has become a center of shipbuilding, and steel, textile, and chemical manufacturing.

Since so much of Italy is coastal, it is natural that the sea should be an important part of the nation's economic life. Seafood of all kinds, from squid to eels, is basic to the Italian diet. Italy's vessels make up one of the world's largest passenger and cargo fleets. Genoa, Naples, and Trieste (Tree-*es*-tay) are important seaports. The fabled city of Venice is literally built in the water, with canals serving as streets and boats as taxis, buses, and trucks.

Archaeological evidence indicates that Italy was inhabited by many peoples even before recorded history. According to legend, the great city of Rome was founded on seven hills about 750 B.C. by the twin brothers, Romulus and Remus. In the beginning, Rome was a kingdom ruled by the Tarquin family. The kingdom was overthrown about 500 B.C., and a kind of republic was started.

Julius Caesar was one of the many great Roman soldier-statesmen who conquered widely and extended the rule of Rome through most of western and central Europe, the Middle East, and North Africa. In 50 B.C.,

Boats of all kinds parade on the Grand Canal in Venice, a city built on more than a hundred islands.

after a major victory in the north, he was ordered not to return to Rome with his army for fear he might take over the country. In defiance, he returned, uttering his now famous statement, "The die is cast." Shortly after his arrival, he was assassinated by conspirators who believed that he wanted absolute power.

Julius Caesar's nephew, Octavian, declared himself Emperor a few years later. His reign is generally considered to be the beginning of what is known as the Golden Age of Rome. During this period, spectacular buildings were built in the city and throughout the provinces. Huge armies were sent out to conquer most of the known world. Latin, the language of Rome, flourished during this time. Great Roman writers include the historian Tacitus, the critic Petronius, the playwright Seneca, and the poets Vergil and Horace. Latin became almost a universal tongue with the spread of the Empire. In the fourth century, the Roman Emperor Constantine embraced Christianity. The Empire and the Church together continued the spread of Latin and Christianity.

The armies of the Empire were stopped by the Germanic tribes of the north. Later, other barbarian tribes came into Italy, including first the Huns from Central Asia and then the Goths. Eventually, they defeated the Roman armies, overran the peninsula, took Rome, and finally destroyed the Italian part of the Empire. All that remained of the great past was the headquarters of the Roman Catholic Church and a strong Roman civilizing influence on the barbarian conquerors.

During the centuries that followed, many separate cities and small states emerged in Italy. In the thirteenth century, the most important was Venice, which ruled much of southern and eastern Europe. But it seemed that no power could unite Italy again. At the end of the fourteenth century, the Renaissance began in Italy and later spread to the rest of Europe. Italy was again important, although it continued as a collection of small kingdoms, principalities, and city-states.

Between 1795 and 1812, Napoleon took over most of the Italian states. His administrators were harsh and failed to unite the country, and strong opposition movements developed. In 1815, when Napoleon was finally defeated, the Italian unification movement began. It was called the *Risorgimento* (the resur-

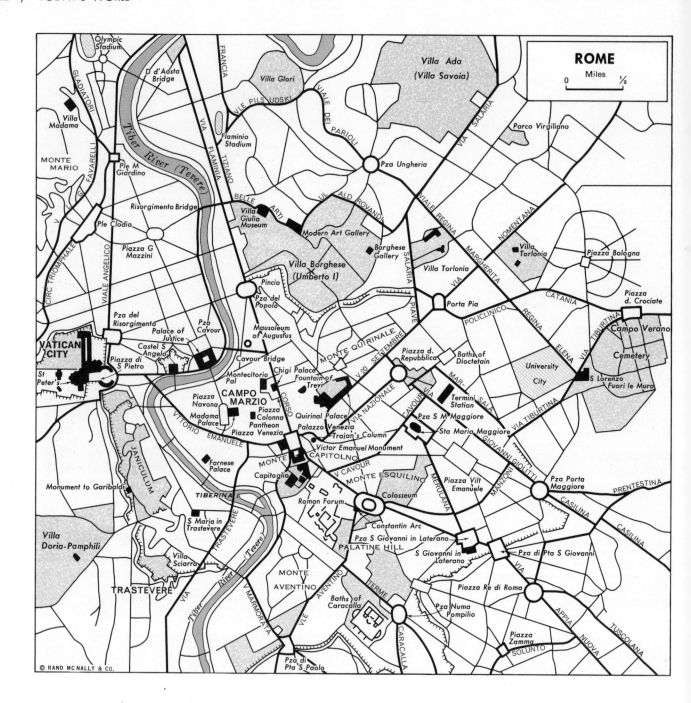

gence). It took until 1870 for the leaders of the movement to reunite most of the states and cities of the
Italian peninsula into one kingdom.

Long a major cultural force in Europe, Italy once
more became a political force. It sided against Austria-
Hungary in World War I, and gained the northern
provinces of Lombardy and Veneto. Shortly after the
war, in 1922, Benito Mussolini and his black-shirted
Fascist Party took over the reins of the country. Mussolini ruled as dictator, and for a decade enjoyed widespread support among world powers. His invasion of
Ethiopia in 1936 and his alliance with Adolf Hitler's
Germany turned the Allied world against him. In 1940,
Italy invaded France from the south as the Germans
were marching in from the north.

Italy itself was invaded by Allied armies and defeated in 1943. Mussolini was executed by the Italians.
A national election ended the monarchy, and Italy became a republic.

Today Italy is no longer a great political power.
But its cultural influence is again being felt. As an
economic power and an active partner in efforts to
unite Europe economically and politically, it works to
insure its future stability.

VATICAN CITY

The magnificent dome of the church of St. Peter dominates the Vatican City.

Lone survivor of the papal states that once occupied central Italy, Vatican City—the world capital of Roman Catholicism—occupies 108 acres in the heart of Rome. Ironically, it stands on the site of Nero's Circus —where Christian martyrs were slain to provide pleasure for Roman mobs. The Vatican is the repository of some of the world's greatest art treasures. The magnificent Basilica of St. Peter is the largest church in the world. On the walls and ceiling of the Sistine Chapel, Michelangelo painted his incomparable frescos. The Pope, religious authority over the world's Roman Catholics, is absolute sovereign of the state, head of its diplomatic service, police force, railway station, and postal system.

The high altar of St. Peter's in Vatican City, focal point of Roman Catholicism and the largest Christian church in the world

SAN MARINO

▲ SEE MAP PAGES 118–119

Capital: San Marino

Population (1962): 17,000

    Density: 739 per square mile

Area: 23 square miles

Elevation: Highest point: 2,425 feet

    Lowest point: 174 feet

Principal language: Italian

Principal religion: Catholicism

Currency unit: Italian Lira

National holiday: October 1, San Marino
    Foundation Day

A postage stamp of mountainous San Marino, the oldest republic in the world

Completely surrounded by Italy, San Marino, the world's oldest republic, nestles in the eastern slope of the Apennines. According to tradition, a Christian stonecutter, Marinus, founded it in the fourth century. In the 1860's, it was the only autonomous state able to resist Italian unification and remain independent.

Agriculture is the main industry. Tourism and the sale of postage stamps bolster the meager national income. The Sanmarinese, as they are called, speak Italian and are Roman Catholics.

MALTA

▲ SEE MAP PAGES 118–119

Capital: Valletta

Population (1962): 330,000

    Density: 2,705 per square mile

    Distribution: Urban: 64 per cent

        Rural: 36 per cent

Area: 122 square miles

Elevation: Highest Point: 817 feet

    Lowest Point: Sea level

Principal languages: English; Maltese

Principal religion: Catholicism

Currency unit: Pound

Malta's strategic importance as a military base for supplies and operations was recognized early. It was the famous stronghold and headquarters of the Crusader Knights of Malta. The symbol they wore is still called a Maltese cross. The largest of a group of islands halfway along the Mediterranean Sea, it has changed hands innumerable times. Since 1814 it has been a British possession, and today still has a great British-NATO naval base. The crown colony of Malta includes Malta itself and two smaller islands, Gozo and Comino. Two uninhabited islets round out the group. Valletta, the capital city on the island of Malta, has one of the world's finest harbors. The islands are rocky. Though many of its people are farmers, most food must be imported. British defense forces are the mainstay of the island's economy. The Maltese people trace their ancestors to a diversity of peoples, including Phoenicians, Greeks, and various western European nationalities. The Maltese language is a hybrid mixture of Arabic and Italian.

GREECE

▲ SEE MAP PAGES 126–127

Capital: Athens

Population (1962): 8,435,000

    Density: 165 per square mile

    Distribution: Urban: 35 per cent

        Rural: 65 per cent

Area: 51,169 square miles

Elevation: Highest point: 9,570 feet

    Lowest point: Sea level

Principal language: Greek

Principal religion: Greek Orthodox

Political divisions: 51 prefectures

Currency unit: Drachma

National holiday: March 25, Independence Day

National anthem: *Ethnikos Hymnos* (The opening line, translated, reads: "Yes, I know thee")

Tobacco leaves curing in Mediterranean sunlight.

On the deeply sculptured land at the tip of the Balkan Peninsula—in what we now call Greece—were sown the seeds of modern Western civilization. Liberty, democracy, scientific inquiry, appreciation of beauty, the concept of the nobility of man—all grew and flourished on this inflexible terrain. The culture of the Greeks at their height reached the ancient world's highest peak of sophistication.

What little we know of the origins of the Greek people indicates that they migrated into the country

On the Acropolis in Athens lie ruins of some of the world's greatest architecture and sculpture, including the Parthenon (right).

GREECE AND ALBANIA

GREECE

Principal Cities

Pop.—Thousands		
20	Agrínion	C 3
6	Aitolikón	C 3
6	Aíyina (Aegina)	D 4
15	Aíyion	C 4
12	Akharaí	g11
17	Alexandroúpolis	B 5
5	Alistráti	B 5
7	Almirós	C 4
15	Amaliás	D 3
12	Amaroúsion	g11
6	Ámfissa	C 4
13	Árgos	D 4
4	Árgos Orestikón	B 3
9	Argostólion	C 3
13	Arta	C 3
5	Asprópirgos	g11
4	Atalándi	C 4
565	Athens (Athínai)	C 4, h11
4	Ayía Paraskeví	C 6
6	Ayiássos	C 6
15	Áyios Dhimítrios	g11
8	Dhidhimótikhon	B 6
29	Dráma	B 5
15	Edhessa	B 4
4	Ekhínos	B 5
6	Elassón	C 4
11	Elevsís (Eleusis)	g11
3	Erithraí	C 4, g10
6	Fársala	C 4
9	Filiatrá	D 3
12	Flórina (Phlorina)	B 3
8	Gargaliánoi	D 6
8	Glifádha	h11
5	Grevená	B 3
6	Ierápetra	E 5
32	Ioánnina	C 3
51	Iráklion (Candia)	E 5
5	Istiaía	C 4
38	Kalámai	D 4
4	Kalampáka	C 3
10	Kálimnos	D 6
47	Kallithéa	h11
19	Kardhítsa	C 3
5	Karlóvasi	D 6
4	Karpenísion	C 3
9	Kastoría	B 3
3	Kástron	C 5
25	Kateríni	B 4
3	Katoúna	C 3
42	Kaválla	B 5
27	Kérkira (Corfu)	C 2
24	Khalkís (Chalcis)	C 4, g11
33	Khaniá (Canea)	E 4
24	Khíos (Chios)	C 6
5	Khrisoúpolis	B 5
12	Kifisiá	g11
10	Kilkís	B 4
4	Kími	C 5
5	Kiparissía	D 3
30	Komotiní	B 5
18	Kórinthos (Corinth)	D 4, h 9
7	Koropí	h11
9	Kós (Cos)	D 6
18	Kozáni	B 3
4	Kranídhion	D 4
22	Lamía	C 4
8	Langadhás	B 4
41	Lárisa (Larissa)	C 4
7	Lávrion	D 5
3	Leonídhion	D 4
11	Levádhia	C 4, g 9
7	Levkás (Leucas)	C 3
3	Límni	C 4
5	Litókhoron	B 4
5	Loutrá Aidhipsoú	C 4
6	Loutrákion	h 9
4	Mándra	C 4, g11
5	Markópoulon	h11
14	Mégara	C 4, g10

Adriatic Sea
Ionian Sea
Gulf of Taranto
Strait of Otranto
YUGOSLAVIA
ALBANIA
ITALY
MACEDONIA
EPIRUS
PINDUS MTS.
THESSALY
IONIAN ISLANDS
PELOPONNESOS
GREECE
Tiranë
Skopje
Bari
Taranto
Brindisi
Lecce
Kérkira
KÉRKIRA (CORFU)
LEVKÁS (LEUCAS)
KEFALLINÍA (CEPHALONIA)
ZÁKINTHOS (ZANTE)
Gulf of Corinth
Pátrai (Patras)
Kalámai
Gulf of Laconia
C. MATAPAN
KÍTHIRA (CYTHERA)
ATTICA
Athens (Athínai)
Piraiévs (Piraeus)
Saronic Gulf
Khalkís (Chalcis)
Thívai (Thebes)
Elevsís (Eleusis)
Mégara
Salamís
Levádhia
Corinth Canal
Kórinthos (Corinth)
1 Inch = 16 Statute Miles
© RM$N&Co.
Statute Miles
Kilometers

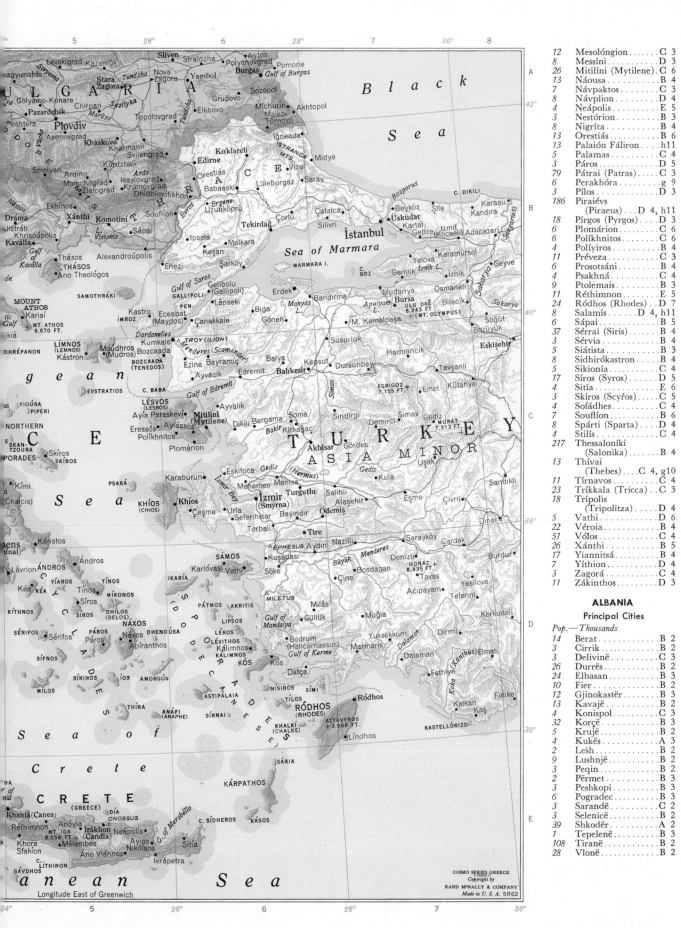

Conic Projection

SCALE 1:4,000,000   1 Inch = 63 Statute Miles

from the Danube Valley more than 4,000 years ago. Very little is known about their occupation of Greece. It is known that they replaced a Mediterranean people who had developed a very high level of civilization in Greece and on the islands—especially on Crete (*Kreet*). The Cretans had at one time established seafaring supremacy in the Mediterranean and developed a trade with Egypt and southwestern Asia.

Greece (Hellas) takes its name from an ancient northern tribe, the Hellenes, but for a long time it referred only to the land occupied by people who spoke Greek. In the centuries before Alexander the Great, there was no unified country called Greece, or Hellas. Communications and trade among the country's mountainous regions were at best difficult. In ancient times, Greece developed as a scattered collection of city-states such as Athens, Sparta (Spartí), and Corinth (Kórinthos). Most grew up in fertile lowlands on or near the sea and became involved in active trade with other Mediterranean lands. Usually each was built around a fortified acropolis, an easily defended rocky hill.

At first the city-states were ruled by kings. Later they evolved into popular democracies, in which citizens exercised the functions of government by majority vote. This was a new idea in government. Early in the history of the city-states, their inhabitants learned nautical skills and embarked on extended voyages for trade and colonization. They founded settlements that became the cities now called Istanbul, in Turkey; Syracuse, in Sicily; Naples, in Italy; and Marseille, in France, to name a few. These colonies became centers of trade and helped to supply Greece with grain and other food.

Philosophy, science, literature, medicine, and sculpture grew with the development of trade. This trade brought great wealth and made possible a class with

GREECE
ECONOMY

SCALE
100 Miles

ECONOMY

HEAVY INDUSTRY
- Machinery
- Transportation Equipment Ship

LIGHT INDUSTRY
- Chemicals
- Food Processing
- Leather Products
- Stone Clay & Glass Products
- Metal Products
- Textiles
- Silk
- Carpets
- Tobacco Products
- Wineries Breweries Distilleries

OTHERS
- Seaport
- Water Power
- Fishing Areas

MINING
- B Bauxite
- Cr Chromite
- Cu Copper
- I Iron Ore
- L Lead
- Li Lignite
- Mg Magnesium
- Z Zinc

AGRICULTURE
- Mediterranean Agriculture
- Seasonal Grazing with Sparse Agriculture
- General Farming
- Forestry with some Farming and Pasture
- Pastureland & Fodder Crops

© RM₅N & CO.

A view of modern Athens, as seen from the Acropolis. The city is built in valleys between rocky hills.

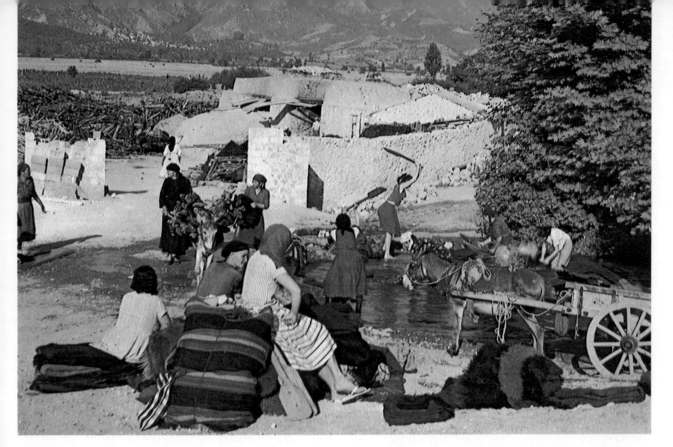

Greek village women washing clothes in a pond. The mountains and valley in the background form a typical Greek landscape.

money and leisure to devote to philosophy and art. Greek thinkers sought rational answers to the secrets of nature. Their accomplishments laid the groundwork for much modern thought. Greek architecture combined structural simplicity with a grandeur of style. It reflected the culture from which it stemmed and left monuments of lasting beauty.

Greek civilization reached its full flowering in the fifth and fourth centuries before Christ. Then the conflicts between the city-states began to weaken them seriously. The disunity of the country invited outside attack. In 338 B.C., Philip of Macedon, king of the region astride the present-day northern border of Greece, swept south with an army and conquered the city-states. On Philip's death, rule over Greece passed to his son, Alexander, then a youth of twenty. By the time of his death thirteen years later, he had led his conquering armies southward to Egypt and eastward as far as the Indus Valley in present Pakistan. He is known to history as Alexander the Great.

Alexander opened a path for Greek civilization into these vast regions, but also paved the way for a backward infusion of other cultures into Greece and the rest of Europe. After Alexander's death his great empire broke up into separate parts ruled by his generals. The Greek city-states recovered some of their prestige, especially in the arts.

Within two hundred years after Alexander's death,

Greece had been absorbed by the expanding Roman Empire. Under Roman rule, Greece recovered much of its former prosperity and enjoyed centuries of peace. In the fourth century A.D., the Roman emperor, Constantine I, divided the Empire into eastern and western sections. As capital of the eastern empire, he chose ancient Byzantium, renaming it Constantinople after himself (*Constantinuo Polis*—Constantine's City—now Istanbul, Turkey). Greece remained part of the Eastern Roman Empire until the Empire was conquered by the Ottoman Turks.

Rising nationalism led to early nineteenth-century insurrection and independence. Except for a short post-World War I period as a republic, Greece has been a monarchy ever since it became independent. Today the king's power is nominal, with the functions of government in the hands of a prime minister and single-house Parliament.

The Greeks have had a beautiful but harsh land to rely upon for sustenance. More than three-quarters of the country rises up in rugged mountain ranges. Only a little more than a quarter of the land can be farmed, and most of the farms are small. The chief crops are wheat, cotton, tobacco, raisins, currants, citrus fruits, and olives. Tobacco is the chief export, followed by currants, olives, and olive oil.

The country's most fertile region is in the north and northeast: Macedonia, Thrace, and part of Thessaly.

Greek children perform a traditional pre-Lenten dance. They are dressed in a kilted costume now worn only as holiday dress.

Here the mountains are interspersed with wide plains. Rainfall is more abundant in the north than elsewhere in Greece, and the land produces large vegetable and grain crops.

Epirus (E-*pie*-rus), which extends inland from the country's northwest coast, is dry and corrugated, of little use agriculturally. Central Greece, just south of Thessaly, has the country's driest climate. On its jutting southeast finger are Athens, the capital, and its port city, Piraeus (Pie-*ree*-us; or Piraiévs).

Southwest of Athens and separated from the main expanse of the country by the Gulf of Corinth, is the Peloponnesus. It is shaped much like a human hand. The currant—a small seedless raisin—takes its name from Corinth, from which it originally came.

Bays and gulfs indent the Greek coast. Studding the Aegean Sea are the beautiful Greek islands. They account for a fifth of the country's total area. Set in an azure sea under a blue Mediterranean sky, the

islands have become one of the country's main tourist attractions. Their inhabitants depend on the sea and on visitors for a livelihood. The island names are familiar to traveler and historian. They are the Cyclades group which includes Páros, Náxos, Ándros, Tínos, Mélos, Dhílos, (Delos), and Sámos; the Sporades (Dodecanese), Khíos (Chios), and Lésvos (Lesbos); Ródhos (Rhodes), and, of course, Crete.

Exploitation of Greece's great mineral wealth is in its infancy, although silver has been mined since ancient times. Lack of coal is offset somewhat by hydro-electric power, but without coal, manufacturing suffers. What industry there is concentrates on textiles, chemicals, foodstuff processing, building materials, and pottery. The number of Greek-owned merchant ships is far out of proportion to the wealth of the country.

The Greek language belongs to a great language family called Indo-European. Nearly all European languages, including English, belong to this same group. Greek was the first of the western Indo-European tongues to be spoken by people with an advanced civilization. The Greek alphabet, based on an alphabet used by Phoenician traders, developed into the Roman alphabet, which we use today, and at a later date was used as a foundation for the alphabet of the eastern Slavs, called Cyrillic.

The Greek language of the Homeric Age—about 800 B.C.—and that of the present resemble each other in basic form. Although a modern Greek can read ancient Greek without special study, he probably would not understand it if he heard it spoken. The influence of Greek in the development of other European tongues has been pervasive. Our word for the twenty-six letters of the English alphabet is taken from *alpha* and *beta*, the names of the first two letters of the Greek alphabet. From *psyche* (soul or mind) we get "psychology" in English. From *arithmo* (I count) comes "arithmetic." *Phone* means sound in Greek, and it comes down to us in "phonetic," and "telephone."

Greece has many attractions for visitors, among them the pleasant Mediterranean climate and great natural beauty of its mountains, valleys, rugged seacoast, and many islands. Greece also has picturesque old towns and villages that have changed little in hundreds of years. Its colorful fishing vessels, especially those in the sponge-fishing fleet, are a delight to tourists. Greatest of all its attractions, however, are its ruins and other reminders of its early history. Many people know something about ancient Greece and come to see the place where so much of European civilization was born.

Today Greece has almost recovered from four years of Nazi occupation during World War II, which caused great hardship throughout the country.

ALBANIA

▲ SEE MAP PAGES 126–127

Capital: Tiranë

Population (1962): 1,680,000

Density: 151 per square mile

Distribution: Urban: 20 per cent;

Rural: 80 per cent

Area: 11,099 square miles

Elevation: Highest point: 9,068 feet;

Lowest point: Sea level

Principal language: Albanian

Principal religions: Islam; Orthodox

Political divisions: 10 prefectures

Currency unit: Lek

National holiday: November 29, Liberation Day

National anthem: *Hymni Flamuri* (The opening line, translated, reads: "To be united behind our flag")

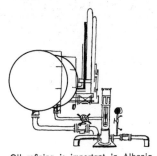

Oil refining is important in Albania.

At various times, Albania has been ruled by Romans, Greeks, Serbs, Venetians, Normans, Turks, Italians, and Germans. But no one was able to control the Albanians completely. Their rugged mountains hid them.

Those mountains contain little fertile soil. Their ruggedness makes recovery of minerals and timber very difficult. The mountains, called the Albanian Alps, are a continuation of the ranges that stretch all the way down the Adriatic seacoast from Italy. There are few lowlands in Albania.

Toward the southern part of the coast, the main crop is corn. In the mountains, the peasants graze sheep and goats to provide wool and mohair, milk, cheese, and some meat. Apart from the coastal plains, the only other highly productive farm area is in the southeast along the Greek border. Wheat, tobacco, olives, figs, and grapes are also widely grown.

Albanians are believed to be the oldest existing nationality in southeastern Europe. They are the descendants of the Illyrians, a people who lived on the Balkan Peninsula during the same period as the ancient Greeks. The Greeks, and later the Serbs and other Slavs, pushed them into isolated mountain areas. The Turks began invading in 1444, and remained in Albania until 1912. The Italians took Albania in 1939 and lost it in 1944. Since then it has been dominated by the local Communists.

A Soviet barge on the Danube River passes the city of Bratislava, Czechoslovakia.

A Hungarian steel mill. Most of Hungary's heavy industries have been developed since World War II.

EASTERN EUROPE

Between Western Europe and the Soviet Union lies a region that has been called the shatter zone. This is the area where eastern and western influences have met throughout recorded history. At present the Iron Curtain lies across this region. West of it is the free world, east of it is the world of communism. An irregular line from the Baltic to the Adriatic represents the westernmost extension of the Slavic peoples. Across this region lies the boundary between the Roman Catholic and the Eastern Orthodox churches—of great historical importance. Here, too, is the line between the Roman alphabet and the eastern alphabets. In the greatest of all barbarian attacks on Europe, the Mongol invasion of 1242, two prongs of the invading hordes reached the Baltic and the Adriatic. Their force was spent in the shatter zone. Later, when the Ottoman Turks pushed into Europe, their westernmost successful conquest was Hungary. They went on to beseige Vienna, but were thoroughly defeated.

The peoples of Eastern Europe have never been able to build strong countries. Some have been successful for a time. Poland once was a kingdom that reached from the Baltic to the Black Sea, but within a few years Poland itself had disappeared from the map. Every one of these countries had at times lost whole provinces to its neighbors. Every one had at some time been wholly conquered and subjected to outside rule. This is a zone in which nationalities have kept their identities, but countries have not been permanent. It is a region that has never been able to reach political maturity because it has never had peace for a long enough time.

Polish soldiers on leave help with the grain harvest.

EUROPE
✪ Capitals

Physical Features

Statute Miles 100 0 100 200 300
Kilometers 100 0 100 200 300 400

Conic Projection
SCALE 1:16,000,000   1 Inch = 252 Statute Miles

BULGARIA

▲ SEE MAP PAGES 138–139

Capital: Sofia

Population (1962): 7,975,000

   Density: 187 per square mile

   Distribution: Urban: 27 per cent

      Rural: 73 per cent

Area: 42,729 square miles

Elevation: Highest point: 9,592 feet

   Lowest point: Sea level

Principal language: Bulgarian

Principal religion: Eastern Orthodox

Political divisions: 27 okrugs; 3 cities

Currency unit: Lev

National holiday: Sept. 9, Liberation Day

National anthem: *Natsionalniyat Khimn* (The opening line, translated, reads: "Dear Bulgaria, land of heroes")

Fine wheat grows on the plains beside the Danube River.

Much of Bulgaria is mountainous. The mountains are beautiful, but they bring little wealth to Bulgaria since they have few natural resources other than forests.

Farms of commercial importance are found on the plateau that lies between the Balkan Mountains and the Danube River, which forms the northern border of the country. Grapes, wheat, barley, flax (the raw material from which linen is made), and sunflowers for oil and feed are grown. Wheat farms cover the northeast

These are Bulgarians harvesting wheat by hand on a collective farm. Farm machinery is needed in much of eastern Europe.

tip of Bulgaria along the Black Sea north of Varna.

Bulgaria's most famous crop can be found on the southern side of the Balkan Mountains. Here thousands of acres are devoted to the growing of roses, from which attar of roses is extracted. It is a vital ingredient of perfume. Even today, women in colorful native dress harvest these flowers by hand. The Maritsa River Valley (Ma-*rit*-sa), in the southeast, is a mild, fertile region that has been compared to California. With enough rainfall or irrigation, its fields can yield two crops a year. Cotton, tobacco, corn, rice, wheat, and fruit are the principal products of this region. Aromatic tobacco is Bulgaria's most important export.

Until recently, the typical Bulgarian farm family lived in a one-room house in the midst of a tiny farm. They were almost self-sufficient. All they bought was salt, coffee, shoes, kerosene for their lamps, and a few other necessities. Since the Communists took over in 1947, they have reorganized nearly all the nation's land into collective farms.

A great industrial change is currently taking place within the country. Traditionally, Bulgarian factories existed simply to process farm products. They made cigarettes, wove textiles, extracted oil and feed from sunflowers, ground wheat into flour, refined sugar beets, and pressed grapes into wine.

Now the government is building factories in an attempt to provide many new jobs for marginal mountain farmers. New towns have been built around new plants where chemicals, building materials, various kinds of machinery, and other nonconsumer products are manufactured. Dimitrovgrad (Di-*mee*-trov-grat) is the largest of the new towns.

Until recently the principal occupations in Bulgaria, aside from farming and factory work, were handicrafts. Bulgarian craftsmanship has been famous for centuries. Products of the craft shops included hand-tooled leather goods, hammered metal containers, and carved and painted wooden objects.

As a nation, modern Bulgaria is less than one hundred years old. Much of the capital city, Sofia (*So*-fee-a), dates from the early twentieth century. The oldest building in the city is a Christian church built in the fourth century. In those days, the land now occupied by Bulgaria was part of the Byzantine Empire, ruled from nearby Constantinople (now called Istanbul).

The people who gave their name to the country, the Bulgars, arrived toward the end of the seventh century. They were a Turkic people from the Volga region in central Russia. They conquered the Slavic inhabitants, intermarried with them, and adopted their language and customs. As a result, the Bulgarian people of today are considered to be basically Slavic. But more than 700,000 Turkish Moslems also live in the country, usually in their own separate villages, each with its mosque and minaret.

Bulgaria became a great power in eastern Europe during the ninth and tenth centuries, but it was finally subdued by the forces of the Byzantine Empire.

In the fourteenth century, the Ottoman Turks came out of Central Asia. Their chief object of conquest was Constantinople, but the city was so well fortified that they by-passed it and marched north into Bulgaria. The Turks ruled Bulgaria until the second half of the nineteenth century.

After first gaining self-rule under Turkey, Bulgaria was given independence under a German king in 1908. During that period, Bulgaria was very friendly with Russia, and the many Russian-style churches in Sofia testify to the closeness of the two countries.

The monarchy continued to rule Bulgaria until after World War II, when the Communists came in.

Even as an Iron Curtain country, Bulgaria remains a nation of fiercely independent, hard-working people. For many of them, the *zadruga*, the peasant clan, is still the final authority.

BULGARIA

ECONOMY

SCALE
50 Miles

ECONOMY

HEAVY INDUSTRY
- Machinery
- Petroleum Refining
- Transportation Equipment Railroad
- Transportation Equipment Ship

OTHERS
- Fishing
- Seaport
- Tourists & Resorts
- Water Power

MINING
- c Coal
- Cu Copper
- I Iron Ore
- L Lead
- u Lignite
- Mn Manganese
- Sa Salt
- Z Zinc

LIGHT INDUSTRY
- Electrical & Electronic Products
- Chemicals
- Food Processing
- Furniture
- Metal Products
- Rubber Products
- Stone Clay & Glass Products
- Textiles
- c Cotton
- Tobacco Products

AGRICULTURE
- Plantation Agriculture
- Intensive Agriculture
- General Farming
- Pastureland & Fodder Crops
- General Farming (Irrigated)
- Forestry with some Farming and Pasture

© RMCN & CO.

YUGOSLAVIA, ROMANIA, HUNGARY, AND BULGARIA

BULGARIA
Principal Cities
Pop.—Thousands

25	Asenovgrad	E	7
22	Blagoevgrad (Gorna Dzhumaya)	D	6
73	Burgas	D	8
16	Chirpan	D	7
34	Dimitrovgrad	D	7
60	Dimitrovo (Pernik)	D	6
33	Gabrovo	D	7
19	Gorna Oryakhovitsa	D	7
31	Kazanlŭk	D	7
39	Khaskovo	E	7
42	Kolarovo	D	8
21	Kŭrdzhali	E	7
25	Kyustendil	D	6
23	Lom	D	7
18	Lovech	D	7
15	Nova Zagora	D	8
14	Panagyurishte	D	7
40	Pazardzhik	D	7
14	Peshtera	D	7
16	Petrich	E	6
58	Pleven	D	7
163	Plovdiv	D	7
18	Razgrad	D	8
83	Ruse	D	7
17	Samokov	D	6
14	Sevlievo	D	7
20	Silistra	C	8
46	Sliven	D	7
612	Sofia (Sofiya)	D	6
25	Stanke Dimitrov (Dupnitsa)	D	6
55	Stara Zagora	D	7
19	Svishtov	D	7
43	Tolbukhin (Dobrich)	D	8
14	Tŭrgovishte	D	8
25	Tŭrnovo	D	7
120	Varna (Stalin)	D	8
24	Vidin	C	6
27	Vratsa	D	6
42	Yambol	D	8

HUNGARY
Principal Cities
Pop.—Thousands

30	Baja	B	4
41	Békéscsaba	B	5
1,807	Budapest	B	4
30	Cegléd	B	4
130	Debrecen	B	5
23	Érd	B	4
35	Eger	B	5
23	Esztergom	B	4
29	Gyöngyös	B	4
71	Győr (Raab)	B	3
27	Hajdúböszörmény	B	5
40	Hódmezővásárhely	B	5
43	Kaposvár	B	3
46	Kecskemét	B	4
23	Kiskunfélegyháza	B	4
30	Makó	B	5
143	Miskolc	A	5
34	Nagykanizsa	B	3
40	Nyíregyháza	B	5
27	Orosháza	B	5
34	Ózd	A	5
26	Pápa	B	3
115	Pécs	B	4
27	Salgótarján	A	4
41	Sopron	B	3
99	Szeged	B	5
56	Székesfehérvár	B	4
25	Szentes	B	5
46	Szolnok	B	5
54	Szombathely	B	3
31	Sztálinváros	B	4
52	Tatabánya	B	4
25	Vác	B	4
25	Veszprém	B	3
24	Zalaegerszeg	B	3

Statute Miles   25   0   25   50   75
Kilometers   25   0   25   50   100

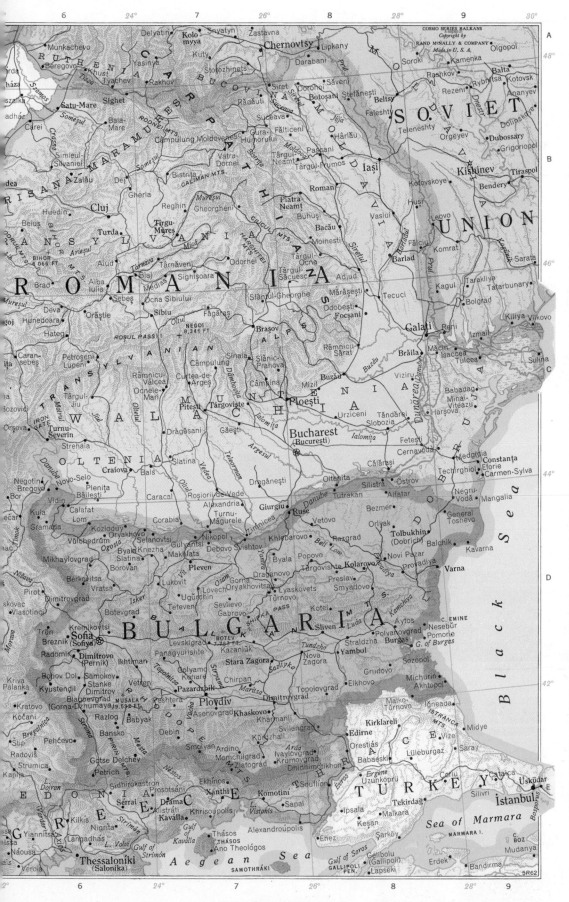

ROMANIA
Principal Cities
Pop.—Thousands

Pop	City	Grid
106	Arad	B 5
54	Bacău	B 8
36	Baia-Mare	B 6
32	Bârlad (Bîrlad)	B 8
20	Bistriţa	B 7
30	Botoşani	B 8
103	Brăila	C 8
124	Braşov (Oraşul-Stalin)	C 7
1,178	Bucharest (Bucureşti)	C 8
48	Buzău	C 8
26	Călărasi	C 8
155	Cluj	B 6
100	Constanţa	C 9
97	Craiova	C 6
28	Focşani	C 8
96	Galaţi (Galacz)	C 8
33	Giurgiu	D 7
36	Hunedoara	C 6
113	Iaşi	B 8
30	Lugoj	C 5
21	Lupeni	C 6
33	Mediaş	B 7
99	Oradea	B 6
23	Petroseni	C 6
38	Piteşti	C 7
115	Ploeşti	C 8
41	Reşita	C 5
28	Roman	B 8
52	Satu-Mare	B 6
90	Sibiu	C 7
22	Sighet	B 7
21	Suceava	B 8
24	Târgovişte	C 7
23	Tecuci	C 8
142	Timişoara	C 5
25	Tulcea	C 9
34	Turda	C 6
32	Turnu-Severin	C 6

YUGOSLAVIA
Principal Cities
Pop.—Thousands

Pop	City	Grid
39	Banja Luka	C 3
23	Bečej	C 5
470	Belgrade (Beograd)	C 5
38	Bitola (Bilolj)	E 5
27	Celje	B 2
32	Karlovac	C 2
30	Kikinda	C 5
42	Kragujevac	D 5
23	Kumanovo	D 5
25	Leskovac	D 5
139	Ljubljana	B 2
81	Maribor	B 2
32	Mostar	D 3
62	Niš	D 5
85	Novi Sad	C 4
59	Osijek	C 4
30	Pančevo	C 5
21	Peć	D 5
31	Pirano	C 1
33	Prilep	E 5
25	Priština	D 5
23	Prizren	D 5
29	Pula (Pola)	C 1
77	Rijeka (Fiume)	C 2
20	Sabac	C 4
136	Sarajevo	D 4
26	Senta	C 5
122	Skopje (Skoplje)	D 5
27	Sombor	C 4
77	Split	D 3
60	Subotica	B 4
20	Tetovo	D 5
32	Tuzla	C 4
20	Vršac	C 5
351	Zagreb	C 2
30	Zenica	C 3
45	Zrenjanin (Petrovgrad)	C 5

YUGOSLAVIA

▲ SEE MAP PAGES 138–139

Capital: Belgrade

Population (1962): 18,700,000
   Density: 189 per square mile
   Distribution: Urban: 15 per cent
       Rural: 85 per cent

Area: 98,776 square miles

Elevation: Highest point: 9,524 feet
   Lowest point: Sea level

Principal languages: Serbo-Croatian; Slovenian; Macedonian

Principal religions: Orthodox; Catholicism; Islam

Political divisions: 6 federated republics

Currency unit: Dinar

National holidays: November 29 and 30, Republic Days

National anthem: *Hej Slaveni* (O, Slavs)

Corn is a leading crop on Yugoslavian farms.

The name Yugoslavia means "land of the South Slavs." Until World War I, the region consisted of two small independent countries, several provinces of Austria-Hungary, and several provinces of Turkey. These countries and provinces were the southernmost homelands of Slavic peoples, which explains the name Yugoslavia. As a result of the war, both the Austro-Hungarian and the Turkish empires broke up, and these various groups of southern Slavs decided to unite in one country. The country was originally called the

This view of Split is characteristic of the Dalmatian coast of Yugoslavia. Mountains rise almost directly from the Adriatic shore.

The interior of a peasant home in mountainous old Montenegro, part of Yugoslavia since the end of World War I. The open fire supplies heat for warmth and cooking. It also smokes the meat hanging from the rafters. The old farmer is playing a primitive, one-stringed instrument called a gusla while his wife works at household tasks.

Kingdom of the Serbs, Croats, and Slovenes. But even that long name left out some of the nation's important parts and peoples.

The northwest part of Yugoslavia, beginning at the Italian frontier, is Slovenia. The Slovenes are Slavic, but their language is distinct from those spoken elsewhere in the country. Much of Slovenia is mountainous, more like northern Italy, Austria, and Switzerland than like any other part of the Balkan Peninsula. Many of the houses resemble Swiss chalets with steep, sloping roofs to hasten the slide-off of heavy winter snows. Like their Alpine neighbors, the Slovenes derive much of their living from cattle raising and forestry.

The western edge of Yugoslavia, called the Dalmatian (Dal-*may*-shun) Coast, presents an entirely different picture. It is composed of a string of rocky peninsulas and islands, with cliffs and outcroppings of limestone. The natives are largely Croatian and speak Serbo-Croat. Fishing is the most important occupation in many of the coastal villages. There is little flat land, and farming is limited mostly to growing olives, figs, and other fruits. The climate is far milder than anywhere else in the country. The town of Split has been

a favored seaside resort for central Europeans for centuries. Dubrovnik (*Doo*-brov-nek), down the coast, is a medieval, walled city that has changed little in more than five hundred years.

Inland from Dalmatia lie the highlands of Serbia and Montenegro (Mon-te-*neg*-ro). Though these mountains are not as high as the Alps, they have few passes through them. As a result, there is little traffic in this large area, and the people are quite isolated. For the most part, they live in poor mountain villages. The only occupation many of the villagers know is grazing sheep and goats in mountain pasturelands.

The region contains some pockets of rich, moist soil. Here the farmers grow corn, wheat, and barley. But these productive fields are usually small and require hand labor. In general, life in this region is hard.

The same may be said of the southern part of Yugoslavia, populated by Albanians (almost as many as live in Albania) and Macedonians. There are also small Greek communities in this region. The single common element here is the widespread evidence of Turkish-Moslem influence. Most of the Albanians and some of the other peoples of the region are Moslems, although the majority are Christian. Almost every

YUGOSLAVIA
ECONOMY

SCALE
75 Miles

ZAGREB
RIJEKA
BELGRADE
SARAJEVO
SKOPJE

ADRIATIC SEA

ECONOMY

HEAVY INDUSTRY
- Machinery
- Iron
- Petroleum Refining
- Transportation Equipment

LIGHT INDUSTRY
- Electrical & Electronic Products
- Chemicals
- Food Processing
- Leather Products
- Lumber & Forest Products
- Metal Products
- Motion Pictures
- Pulp & Paper Products
- Stone Clay & Glass Products
- Textiles
- Carpets
- Tobacco Products
- Wineries Breweries Distilleries
- Jewelry

OTHERS
- Seaport
- Water Power

MINING
- An Antimony
- Ab Asbestos
- B Bauxite
- C Coal
- Cr Chromite
- Cu Copper
- G Gold
- I Iron Ore
- L Lead
- Li Lignite
- Mn Manganese
- Mr Mercury
- Mo Molybdenum
- Pm Petroleum
- Py Pyrite
- S Silver
- Z Zinc

AGRICULTURE
- Mediterranean Agriculture
- Plantation Agriculture
- Intensive Agriculture
- General Farming
- Pastureland & Fodder Crops
- Seasonal Grazing, with Sparse Agriculture
- Forestry with some Farming and Pasture
- Non-Agricultural Areas

© RM℠N & CO.

River. Near the source of the Morava is the source of the Vardar River, which flows southeast to enter the Aegean Sea near Thessaloniki, Greece. Together, the valleys of the Morava and Vardar form a cut that almost makes a highway from the Danube to the Aegean. In this valley of rich orchards, fruit is the principal crop, and pigs are the principal livestock.

Belgrade, on the banks of the Danube, is the capital of Yugoslavia. It is a fairly modern city. Mosques and other signs of Islam crop up throughout the city. The food of Belgrade, as in other parts of Yugoslavia, includes many Middle Eastern dishes such as kebabs, pilaf, and baklava. Also common in Belgrade are pastries and other distinctly Viennese foods, a reminder of the days when the region was ruled by the Austrian Empire.

When Yugoslavia was formed after World War I, the Serbs were the dominant group in the nation. Serbia had been an independent country before World War I, and the king of the new nation had been king of Serbia. The Serbs tried hard, but with little success, to make the entire nation Serbian. They attempted to popularize the Serbian language, which is almost identical with Croatian, except that it uses the Russian-style alphabet instead of the Latin. They also tried to spread Greek Orthodox Christianity in opposition to Roman Catholicism, which prevails in Croatia and Slovenia. Their rigid, centralized government permitted little freedom of action. The intolerance of the Serbian rulers antagonized non-Serbs.

During World War II, the rivalry between the diverse peoples continued. Finally, however, a large underground army was established, and all the peoples of Yugoslavia were invited to join and fight the Nazis. It was led by the Communist leader, Josip Broz Tito. When the war ended, Tito took over. Since then, Yugoslavia has been a Communist nation. But unlike its neighbors in eastern Europe, it has managed to remain independent of the Soviet Union.

After World War II, Yugoslavia began working hard to increase the output of its factories and mines. Coal, lead, and bauxite are among the valuable minerals of the country. Rivalry between the peoples has been reduced. Tito is a Croat, but many of his aides have been Serbs, Montenegrins, and others.

Yugoslavia is now organized as a federal government of six state republics: Serbia, Croatia, Slovenia, Bosnia-Hercegovina, Montenegro, and Macedonia. Each group is allowed to keep its own language and customs. Most of the real power, however, has remained in the hands of the Communist government in Belgrade. Most of the country's resources have been used to make it strong and independent of both the Soviet Union and the Western powers.

village includes a Moslem mosque with its minaret, the distinctive, slender tower from which the muezzin calls the faithful to prayer. Everywhere, local crafts and architecture, with geometric and filigreed patterns, show traces of Moslem heritage. Even the heavy mustaches worn by many of the peasants are considered a holdover from the days of Turkish rule.

The richest area in Yugoslavia lies in the northeast. It is part of the broad Danube Basin, which Yugoslavia shares with Hungary and Romania. The Sava and Drava river valleys are other important, fertile lowlands in this area. The principal crops raised here are wheat, barley, corn, and sugar beets. Within the population are large Hungarian, Romanian, and German-speaking minorities. Sometimes whole towns are inhabited by one or another of these groups.

Entering the Danube from the south is the Morava

ROMANIA

▲ SEE MAP PAGES 138–139

Capital: Bucharest

Population (1962): 18,700,000

   Density: 204 per square mile

   Distribution: Urban: 23 per cent

      Rural: 77 per cent

Area: 91,698 square miles

Elevation: Highest point: 8,346 feet

   Lowest point: Sea level

Principal languages: Romanian; Hungarian

Principal religion: Orthodox

Political divisions: 16 regions

Currency unit: Leu

National holiday: August 23, Liberation Day

National anthem: *Imnul de Stat* (The opening line translated, reads: "We Praise Thee, Fatherland Romania")

Oil from the Ploesti oil fields is Romania's most valuable export product.

Romania has two assets that should make it rich: fertile black soil and large deposits of petroleum. But it also has two liabilities: not enough capital to de- develop the resources and too few trained people.

Europe's great wheat fields begin in the southwest corner of Romania just beyond the point where the Danube flows into the Romanian plains, and extend across the southern part of the country north of the Danube and from there north to the border of the Soviet Union.

Poultry market in Bucharest. Even in the capital, Romanian farmers sell their own products directly to consumers.

ROMANIA

ECONOMY

SCALE
100 Miles

ECONOMY

HEAVY INDUSTRY

- Machinery
- Petroleum Refining
- Transportation
- Equipment

OTHERS

- Seaport
- Water Power
- Insurance

LIGHT INDUSTRY

- Electrical & Electronic Products
- Furniture
- Pulp & Paper Products
- Textiles
- Chemicals
- Leather Products
- Rubber Products

- c Cotton
- Food Processing
- Metal Products
- Stone Clay & Glass Products
- s Silk
- Tobacco Products
- Wineries Breweries Distilleries

MINING

- B Bauxite
- C Coal
- Cu Copper
- G Gold
- I Iron Ore
- l Lead
- Li Lignite
- Mn Manganese
- Gs Natural Gas
- Pm Petroleum
- Sa Salt
- Z Zinc

AGRICULTURE

- Intensive Agriculture
- General Farming
- Pastureland & Fodder Crops
- Forestry with some Farming and Pasture
- Swamp Land

© RMcN & CO.

Transylvania, the part of Romania west of the Carpathians and north of the Transylvanian Alps, also has fertile farmlands that yield various grains, including corn and wheat, and support orchards and vineyards. Flocks of sheep graze in the lower fields through the winters and far into highlands in summer. The farms of Transylvania are productive and profitable because of skillful farming and more rain than falls in the lowland south and east. Experts believe that the farms in the south and east could also be more productive despite occasional droughts and generally light rainfall.

The rich oil fields of Ploesti (Plo-*yesht*) and Câmpina (*Kum*-pee-nah), in the foothills of the Transylvania Alps, present another problem for the nation. Outmoded methods of removing the oil and natural gas caused great waste, and it seemed that the supply may have been exhausted. Recently, modern deep-drilling techniques and efficient extracting methods have been introduced and the fields are now producing at higher levels.

The Romanians are a proud people who trace their ancestry back to the ancient Romans. In the second and third centuries A.D., the area that is now Romania was the Imperial Roman province of Dacia. The present name of the country means "land of the Romans," and the Romanian language stems from Latin and is related to other Romance languages.

Romanians are justly proud of their capital city, Bucharest. Though a fort or village of some kind had existed on the site for centuries, the present city is young and modern. Many of its churches, large public buildings, wide boulevards, and spacious parks were built in the second half of the nineteenth century, and many others were built in the 1930's and after World War II. In Eastern Europe, Bucharest has been known as the Paris of the Balkans.

Like the people of Paris and New York, Bucharest citizens love the theater. There are twenty theaters in the city. Another popular pastime of the Romanians is going to the seashore. The Black Sea coast has many miles of sand beach and a variety of colorful resorts.

Romania gained complete independence in 1878. When the Roman Empire fell into decline after the fourth century A.D., the troops who had been used to hold off the barbarians in the provinces were called home to defend Rome. This opened the way for invaders, among them the Huns, the Goths, and the Mongols, who swept into Romania, pillaging and murdering. Though the Romanians were unable to protect themselves, they kept alive their Roman language. When the Mongols finally departed in the thirteenth century, two small Romanian states came into being, Walachia (Wa-*lah*-kee-uh) in the south and Moldavia (Mol-*day*-vee-uh) in the east. At that time Transylvania was part of Hungary.

In the fifteenth century, Turkish armies invaded the two states, but the Turks allowed the Romanian princes to rule for them. This produced many new rivalries, intrigues, revolts, and alliances with the Hungarians, the Russians, the Poles, the Austrians, and the German emperors.

Through all these ups and downs, the Romanians retained not only their language, but their deep pride in being Romanians. Their goal of national independence was finally achieved when the Turkish Empire began to weaken in the nineteenth century.

Independence did not bring peace to the Romanians. They fought many wars over border territories. Little time or energy was spent on developing a modern land with a modern system of education. As a result, many of the older Romanians cannot read or write, though most of them know by heart their folk tales and songs. Compulsory education laws have been enacted since World War II. In 1947, a Communist regime took over and proclaimed the Romanian People's Republic.

HUNGARY

▲ SEE MAP PAGES 138–139

Capital: Budapest

Population (1962): 10,065,000

    Density: 280 per square mile

    Distribution: Urban: 38 per cent

        Rural: 62 per cent

Area: 35,919 square miles

Elevation: Highest point: 3,330 feet

    Lowest point: 280 feet

Principal language: Hungarian

Principal religions: Catholicism; Protestantism

Political divisions: 19 counties; 5 county boroughs

Currency unit: Forint

National holiday: April 4, Liberation Day

National anthem: *Isten aldd meg a magyart* (God Bless the Hungarians)

Modern tractors are manufactured in government-owned Hungarian factories.

Hungary is the only country in eastern Europe that is not mountainous. Most of Hungary is a great, level plain. With no mountains to protect the country, it has been a prize of conquerors from its earliest history. In the ninth century a people called Magyars swept in from Asia. They were probably related to the Turks, and their language belonged to a group known as Ugrian. The Finns of northern Europe speak a similar language. The Magyars conquered the Slavs of the land that is now Hungary and set up a kingdom about the year 1,000.

There have been many later invasions and wars and a considerable mixture with the Slavs and other European peoples, but the people of Hungary still call themselves Magyars and speak the non-Slavic Magyar language. Because many Hungarians have swarthy complexions and high cheekbones, it was natural to connect them with the Mongols, but authorities now deny this link. In spite of the name of their country, the Hungarians are not related to the Huns.

Hungary is located in the heart of eastern Europe. It is mainly a broad, fertile plain, the largest in this part of Europe. The Danube River cuts through this plain. It is easy to see why so many peoples coveted this land.

The country to the west of the Danube is hilly and gets considerable rainfall. It is the most productive farmland of all. The land to the east, slightly less fertile, is flatter and drier. Farmers on both sides of the river produce wheat, corn, sugar beets, and hogs. They also raise a distinctive variety of white cattle. The cows do not give as much milk as many other breeds, but they thrive on far less water than cattle usually require. The white cattle also make excellent draft animals, an important asset, since many Hungarian farms are still without modern farm machinery.

A vegetable street market in Budapest, where Hungarian farmers are permitted to sell their surplus production.

Budapest, the capital of Hungary, consists of Buda (foreground), on the low side of the Danube River, and Pest, on the hilly side.

In the western part of Hungary is a long, narrow body of water called Balaton Lake. It is shallow, but in area it is the largest lake of Central Europe. Northwest of the lake is the Bakony Forest, a range of low mountains. The steepest slopes face southeast, toward the lake. These slopes are warmed by the sun and have a very pleasant climate. The area has many popular resorts along the lake. Grapes grow on the warm slopes.

Eastern Hungary is a treeless grassland called the Alföld (*Ul*-fuld), or Plain. Most of it is under cultivation. One area, the puszta or prairie, has been compared with the American West. On these naturally dry lands live the Csikos, the Hungarian equivalent of cowboys, who work on ranches where herds of beautiful horses are raised.

Science is changing life habits in the area. A dam built on the Tisza River (*Ti*-su), buttressed by a system of canals, is now supplying water to this hitherto parched area. As a result, the dry grassland is turning into rich fields. The Csikos are becoming rice and cotton farmers. These crops are new to Hungary.

The Magyars were not the first invaders of Hungary, but they were the first to settle. From their base camp on the Hungarian plain, they conducted raids all over Europe. So fierce and devastating were their attacks that the Holy Roman Emperor Otto I declared them "the enemies of God and humanity" and led a crusade against them. In 955 A.D., they were finally beaten in Germany and forced to retreat to Hungary and settle down. They adopted Christianity and began to build a nation. As their kingdom grew, it included not only the area of present-day Hungary, but also lands which are now the northern part of Yugoslavia, the western part of Romania, and Slovakia in what is now the eastern half of Czechoslovakia.

In the thirteenth century, the Mongols charged through the land on their surge of conquest from Central Asia. They nearly destroyed Hungary, but they did not stay long. Shortly after they withdrew their armies, the Magyars again began to prosper, and in the latter half of the fifteenth century, Hungary became one of the strongest nations in Europe.

Invading Turks, pushing toward Vienna, ended Hungarian prosperity. After hard fighting, the Turks finally broke through the Hungarian defense lines onto the plains. In 1526 they defeated the Hungarian army in the Battle of Mohács (*Mo*-hach), a small town in southern Hungary.

As they moved through the plain, the Turks laid waste the country and killed many farmers. They were finally stopped by Austrian armies. The Austrians saved a section of northwestern Hungary from the Turks. As

HUNGARY

ECONOMY

Artisan shops play an important role
in the Hungarian Economy

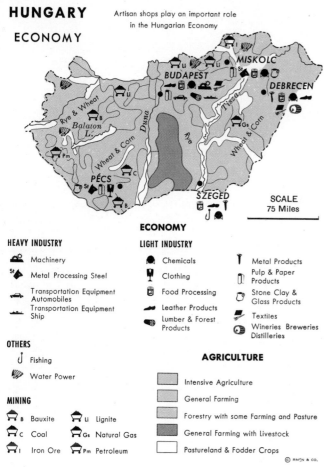

ECONOMY

HEAVY INDUSTRY

- Machinery
- St Metal Processing Steel
- Transportation Equipment Automobiles
- Transportation Equipment Ship

OTHERS

- Fishing
- Water Power

MINING

- B Bauxite
- C Coal
- I Iron Ore
- Li Lignite
- Gs Natural Gas
- Pm Petroleum

LIGHT INDUSTRY

- Chemicals
- Clothing
- Food Processing
- Leather Products
- Lumber & Forest Products
- Metal Products
- Pulp & Paper Products
- Stone Clay & Glass Products
- Textiles
- Wineries Breweries Distilleries

AGRICULTURE

- Intensive Agriculture
- General Farming
- Forestry with some Farming and Pasture
- General Farming with Livestock
-Ranchland & Fodder Crops

© RMCN & CO.

SCALE
75 Miles

---

the Turks were slowly driven back, more and more of Hungary was added to the Austrian Empire, which was later called the Austro-Hungarian Empire or Austria-Hungary.

Many of the farms of central Hungary remained vacant for years after the Turks passed through. Recovery came many years later. In the seventeenth and eighteenth centuries, as the Austrian armies pushed the Turks back, German colonists came in to reclaim the vacant, but fertile, countryside.

Hungary regained much of its former strength, its land, and its importance in Europe. But it remained under the rule of the Austrian Hapsburg family until after World War I.

In 1919 Hungary became independent of Austrian rule. But it also lost about two-thirds of its territory and population. As a result, Hungary today is one of the smaller nations of Europe. Yet it has Budapest, one of the great European capitals, as a sign of its former greatness. The capital was once two separate cities, Buda on the high western bank of the Danube, and Pest, on the flat eastern side. These two, plus some suburbs, were combined to create Budapest in 1873. But even now the people still talk about Buda or Pest.

Before World War I, Budapest was Europe's center for grain trading as well as its largest flour-milling center. It was also long an important point for the processing of other agricultural products of the fertile plains of eastern Europe. Brewing, tanning, sugar-refining, and wine production were among its major industries. Other important industries made Budapest one of Europe's major industrial centers. There are now steel mills and factories that produce chemicals, textiles, and machine tools.

Budapest is much better known in the West for things other than factory products. It is the city of gypsy violin music, of winding streets and ancient houses in the old part of the city, and of geranium-decorated inns and fine restaurants. Hungary, and especially Budapest, are famous also for the spiciness of Magyar food, which almost always includes onions and paprika.

Debrecen (*Deb*-ret-sen) is another important Hungarian city. It is located in the northeast. It was long a center of Protestantism, as well as headquarters for the Hungarian independence movement against Austria.

Szeged (*Se*-ged) is the major city of the great plains. It is located in the south, on the Tisza River. In 1879, that river flooded its banks and destroyed almost the entire city. A brand new town was laid out and built with the aid of contributions from other cities throughout Europe. To show their gratitude, the people of Szeged named many of their broad new streets after the cities that helped them.

Though Hungary has few minerals and little hydroelectric power, it is gaining in importance as a manufacturing nation. New industries use imported raw materials and mainly imported fuels. The government increasingly sponsors programs to explore and develop more domestic resources. Since 1946, the share of the population living and working on farms has fallen sharply.

The Communist Party, under Soviet control, has held Hungary in an iron grip since the end of World War II. The Communists have launched a major program of factory building in new towns all over the countryside. Besides converting a rural land into a richer manufacturing society, the Communists hope the new factory jobs and consumer goods will induce the people to favor Communism.

The Hungarians' feeling of anti-Communism was expressed strongly during the bitter fall days of 1956. The people rose up and actually won the government back for a few days. Then Russian troops smashed the rebellion and brought the Communists back to power. That revolt was a landmark in the battle against Communism and one more landmark in the historic struggle Hungarians have made against outside domination.

CZECHOSLOVAKIA

▲ SEE MAP PAGES 150–151

Capital: Prague

Population (1962): 13,800,000

    Density: 280 per square mile

Distribution: Urban: 27 per cent

        Rural: 73 per cent

Area: 49,366 square miles

Elevation: Highest point: 8,737 feet

    Lowest point: 432 feet

Principal languages: Czech; Slovak

Principal religion: Roman Catholicism

Political divisions: 10 regions (kraj) and capital, Prague

Currency unit: Crown

National holiday: October 28, Nationalization Day

National anthems: Czech; *Kde domov muj?* (Where Is My Native Land?)

    Slovak; *Nad tatrou sa blýska* (Lightning over the Mountains)

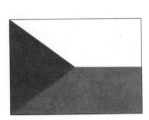

Brewing remains an art in Czechoslovakia.

In his musical epic "My Fatherland," the Bohemian composer Friederich Smetana describes the course of the river Moldau (*Mole*-dow; or Vltava, *Vul*-tah-vah) as a dashing mountain brook, a stream winding through meadowland and town, then as a river flowing to its meeting with the Elbe, and then to its final union with the North Sea. The land through which the Moldau meanders is Czechoslovakia, a small nation, about the size of North Carolina, in the heart of Europe.

Czechoslovakia also claims part of the musically

Prague, in Bohemia province of Czechoslovakia, and the nation's capital, is an important cultural and commercial center.

celebrated—though seldom "blue"—Danube. This river forms part of the border with Austria and Hungary and finally flows into the Black Sea. The Oder gives the landlocked nation an outlet to a third sea: it crosses Poland to the north and empties into the Baltic. Barges and river boats ply these and other water routes, laden with the products of Czechoslovakia's fields and factories to be sold abroad. Their valleys connect widely separated sections of the country, and they generate power for industry.

The mountain barriers within the country and along its frontiers are not very high. The greatest elevation is in the Tatras, on the northeast border with Poland. Farther east the boundary is a range of the Carpathians, the sixty-one-mile border with the Soviet Union. The Sudetes (Soo-*dee*-tees) complete the boundary with Poland, while the Ore Mountains and the Bohemian Forest mark the frontiers with Germany. The mountains are covered with timber and make up a third of the national territory, providing lumber, pulp and paper.

Mountains also seperate the Czech and Slovak regions which give the country its name. West of the White Carpathians and Little Carpathians, which cross the center of the country, are the rolling hills and fields of the Czech districts, Bohemia and Moravia-Silesia. To the east is smaller, mountainous Slovakia.

The Czechs (more than two-thirds of the population of the country) and the Slovaks are both Slavic peoples who speak related tongues. They settled in their present territory during the eighth century, displacing Germanic tribes who had lived there earlier. The history of the area is confusing, with many changes of rulers. Moravia, including Bohemia, became a duchy in Charlemagne's empire, but he had little control over it. In the ninth century the Bohemians and Moravians were converted to Christianity by missionaries from the east, but soon came under the control of the Roman Church. In 874 a strong Moravian ruler set up an independent Kingdom of Great Moravia, which included Bohemia and Slovakia. It lasted only until 906, when it was overthrown.

Bohemia next rose to power and became a strong kingdom in the western part of what is now Czechoslovakia, with its capital at Prague. One of its kings was St. Wenceslaus—the good king of the Christmas carol. Moravia was included in the kingdom, which became one of the states within the Holy Roman Empire. Hungary still held Slovakia, east of Moravia.

In 1403 a young priest, John Huss, was condemned

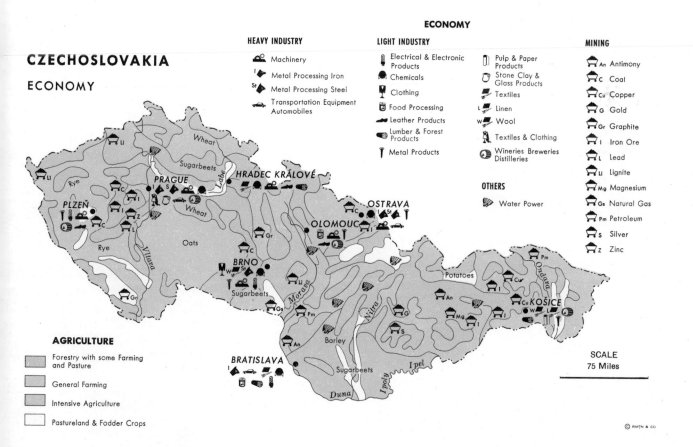

CZECHOSLOVAKIA
Principal Cities

Pop.—Thousands

22	Banská Bystrica	D 5
15	Beroun	D 2, o17
263	Bratislava	D 4
26	Břevnov	n17
315	Brno	D 4
66	České Budějovice	D 3
22	Cheb	C 2
35	Chomutov	C 2
16	Chrudim	D 3
37	Děčín	C 3
30	Dejvice	n17
27	Frýdek-Místek	D 5
60	Gottwaldov (Zlín)	D 4
18	Hodonín	D 4
58	Hradec Králové	C 4
27	Jablonec nad Nisou	C 3
37	Jihlava	D 3
45	Karlovy Vary	C 2
46	Karviná	D 5
52	Kladno	C 3, n17
22	Kolín	C 3
26	Komárno	E 5
85	Košice	D 6
18	Košíře	n17
94	Královské Vinohrady	n17
23	Krnov	C 4
22	Kroměříž	D 4
16	Levice	D 5
69	Liberec	C 3
16	Lučenec	D 5
16	Michalovce	D 6
26	Mladá Boleslav	C 3, n18
43	Most	C 2
19	Náchod	C 4
33	Nitra	D 5
24	Nové Zámky	E 5
17	Novy Jičín	D 5
63	Nusle	n17
77	Olomouc	D 4
44	Opava	D 4
237	Ostrava	D 5
58	Pardubice	C 3
20	Piešťany	D 4
21	Písek	D 3
139	Plzeň	D 2
18	Podmokly	C 3
999	Prague (Praha)	C 3, n17
28	Přerov	D 4
35	Prešov	D 6
21	Příbram	D 3
35	Prostějov	D 4
24	Ružomberok	D 5
62	Smíchov	n17
20	Spišská [Nová Ves]	D 6
22	Šumperk	D 4
20	Tábor	D 3
41	Teplice	C 2
20	Třebíč	D 3
25	Trenčín	D 5
35	Trnava	D 4
24	Trutnov	C 3
26	Turčiansky Sväty Martin	D 5
68	Ústí nad Labem	C 3
16	Varnsdorf	C 3
44	Vršovice	n17
19	Vsetín	D 5
18	Vysočany	n17
16	Žatec	C 2
34	Žilina	D 5
92	Žižkov	n17
24	Znojmo	D 4
22	Zvolen	D 5

POLAND
Principal Cities

Pop.—Thousands

39	Będzin	g10
95	Białystok	B 7
25	Bielawa	C 4
67	Bielsko-Biała	D 5, h10

COSMO SERIES POLAND, CZECH.
Copyright by
RAND McNALLY & COMPANY
Made in U.S.A.

1937 Boundaries Defining Danzig a
German Areas placed under Polish or Russi
Administration by the Potsdam Agreement

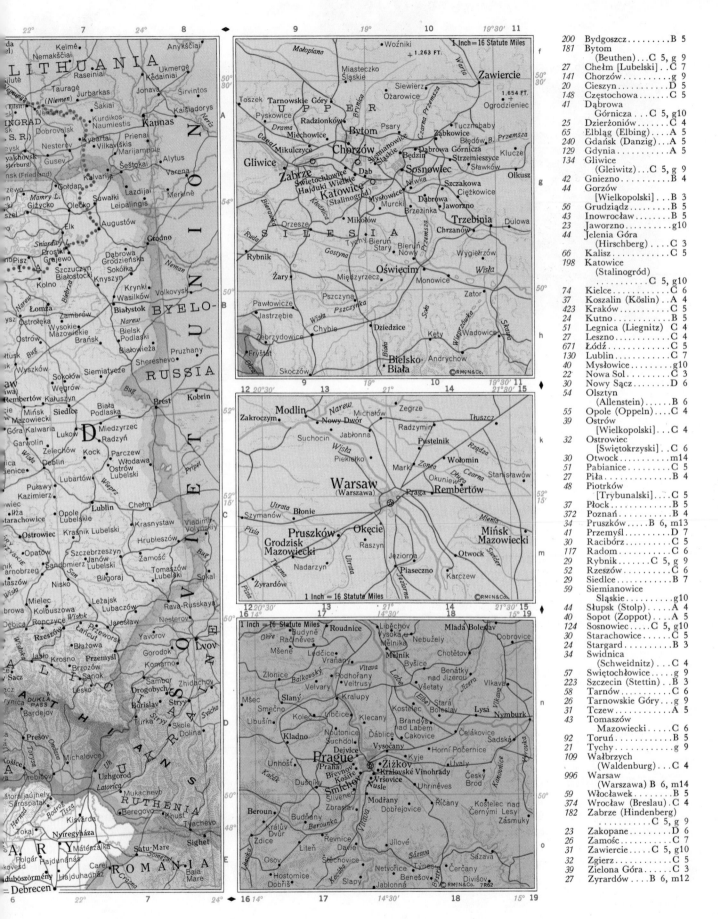

Women help the men in the fields on Czechoslovakian farms. The grain is shoveled into sacks and then weighed.

by the church and the empire for advocating drastic reforms. He soon gained a following among the Czech peasants. Many nobles also supported the Hussites against the German merchants and the king, who had encouraged German immigration. The controversy thus had both a religious and nationalist basis. Huss was burned at the stake, and in 1419, riots in Prague were climaxed when Hussites threw the mayor out a city hall window. At hearing the news the king died in a fit of rage. A civil war broke out over his succession, The Hussite wars lasted for nearly sixty years. Many of the followers of Huss returned to the Church. Today, three-fourths of the Czechoslovaks are Roman Catholics, and nearly a quarter are Hussite Protestants.

The wars of the fifteenth century weakened the Bohemian throne, enabling Ferdinand I of Austria in 1556 to gain control of Bohemia, Moravia, and Hungary, including Slovakia. In 1618, Hussites demanding religious freedom reverted to their novel form of revolt by throwing two Austrian councillors out the window of Hradcany Castle. In 1620, the Bohemians suffered a disastrous defeat and came under the control of Austria. Slovakia was still held by Hungary. These three provinces remained under the Austro-Hungarian Empire until it was dissolved in 1918 as a result of defeat in World War I. Then, for the first time in 1,000 years, they were reunited as the Republic of Czechoslovakia.

Centuries of attempted Germanization of the Czechs and the Slovaks by their Austrian rulers failed to extinguish their national spirit. Under the presidency of Thomas Masaryk, the "Father of Czechoslovakia," the new nation acquired an importance and prosperity that surpassed any chapter of its earlier history.

The independence of the republic lasted only twenty years, however. In 1938 Germany under Hitler demanded the Sudetenland, a border district of Bohemia with a heavy German population. In World War II, which soon followed, Czechoslovakia was swallowed up by Germany. The liberating American and Russian troops met in Czechoslovakia at the war's end, but the Americans withdrew, leaving Soviet influence dominant.

When the Czechoslovakian Republic was re-established after the war, the Communists were the strongest party. Jan Masaryk, the country's foreign minister and son of the founder, who opposed the Communists, met his death by jumping or being thrown out of a window. The Communists took over the country by a coup in 1948. Since then Czechoslovakia has been a Communist state. Unlike the other satellite countries, Czechoslovakia suffered relatively little damage in the war. Its highly developed industry and agriculture make it the most prosperous member of the Communist bloc.

About one-third of the workers of the nation are in manufacturing industries. Coal and iron mines in Bohemia supply most of the national needs. Sometimes additional coal is imported from Poland. Excellent engineering and highly skilled labor compensate for a scarcity of iron ore. Valuable deposits of antimony, silver, and mercury are found in Bohemia. Graphite is exploited to make the country a leading pencil producer. The precious mineral of the atomic age, uranium, is mined at Jachymov (*Yah*-khi-mof) in the Ore Mountains and sold to the USSR.

The cities of Czechoslovakia boast a highly diversified production, now almost entirely nationalized. Heavy industry has traditionally been centered in the Czech regions, but since the war Slovakia has become increasingly industrialized. Automobiles, aircraft, railroad equipment, power plants and food-processing machinery—as well as fine gloves—are manufactured in Prague. It is the capital of Bohemia and of Czechoslovakia and has about a million inhabitants. Brno (*Bur*-no) is the next largest city and the capital of Moravia. It is a trade center and the hub of the textile, clothing, and food industries. Brno is also an important producer of firearms. The capital of Slovakia is Bratislava, which, under its old name of Pressburg, was once capital of Hungary. Manufacture of agricultural machinery, oil, refining, and chemical processing are important industries. Ostrava (*Oh*-strah-vah), near the Moravian coal fields, produces steel, heavy machinery, and chemical products. Plzen (*Pul*-zen-ya; or Pilsen, *Pil*-sen), in western Bohemia, has many kinds of heavy industries, among others a huge arms and munitions plant. Its factories also make airplanes, locomotives, and electrical machinery.

Bohemian glass is one of the traditional products for which Czechoslovakia has long been famed around the world. It is made in many places. Shoes, made at Gottwaldov (Zlín) in Moravia, and the famed beers of Pilsen and Ceské Budejovia (*Che*-skay *Boo*-dye-yo-vit-se; or Budweis), are other Czech products well-known abroad..

Czechoslovakia imports raw materials and semi-prepared foodstuffs, processes them in its factories, and exports the finished goods. Heavy machinery has become a far more important export than the traditional products of light industry since World War II. Trade has shifted, too, from the West to a concentration with the Soviet bloc.

A mild climate, with plentiful rainfall in spring and summer, favors Czech agriculture. About one-third of the working population and a little more than one-half of the territory are devoted to farming, which is largely a state-controlled enterprise. On the fertile rolling Bohemian and Moravian lowlands and along

The Skoda iron and steel works in Czechoslovakia are among the largest in easten Europe. Automobiles are made here.

the black-earth Danube plain in Slovakia, wheat, rye, barley, oats, and potatoes are the principal crops. Sugar beets and hops for the beers of Bohemia are industrial crops. All kinds of livestock are raised and supply the meat for the delicious Czech sausages.

Before the war, people from all over the world came to the resorts of the Czech countryside. At Karlovy Vary (*Kar*-low-ve *Va*-re; or Karlsbad) and Mariánské Lázně (*Mah*-ree-ahn-skay *Lahz*-nye; or Marienbad) in Bohemia, mineral springs noted for their health-giving properties, attracted tourists. They filled the comfortable hotels and thronged the flag-decked promenades beside sparkling fountains. Today these resorts are state-run rest centers for working people.

POLAND

▲ SEE MAP PAGES 150–151

Capital: Warsaw

Population (1962): 30,265,000
    Density: 251 per square mile
    Distribution: Urban: 34 per cent
               Rural: 66 per cent

Area: 120,359 square miles

Elevation: Highest point: 8,212 feet
    Lowest point: 6 feet below
               sea level

Principal language: Polish

Principal religion: Catholicism

Political divisions: 22 provinces (voivodships)

Currency unit: Zloty

National holiday: July 22, National Holiday

National anthem: *Jeszcze Polska nie Zginela*
    (Poland Is Not Yet Forsaken)

Machinery in a Warsaw automobile factory.

In Polish, *pol* means field, and Poland is well named. The country is one vast rolling field, walled along the border with Czechoslovakia to the south by the Sudetes (Soo-*dee*-tees) and Carpathian Mountains and washed in the north by the Baltic Sea. Nu-

merous rivers flow across the plain, emptying into the Baltic, and more than 9000 lakes dot the marshy northern provinces of Pomerania and Masuria. The Oder and Neisse (Nye-se) rivers form most of the western border with East Germany, while the Bug River marks a section of Poland's eastern border with Byelorussia, the adjoining part of the Soviet Union. The Wista (Vistula) flows the entire length of the country, from the Carpathians to the Gulf of Danzig and is linked by canals to the other important rivers. Barges and steamers ply its course, bearing traffic from Warsaw, Poland's capital, to Gdansk (Gu-*dah*-nyusk; or Danzig), on the Baltic.

In winter Poland is bleak and cold, but during the warm and rainy summer the fields are green with crops and pasture. Rainfall varies from less than 20 inches per year on the plains to more than 60 inches

Polish children gather potatoes behind a horse-drawn digger. Potatoes are a leading crop on the plains of northern Poland.

in the higher mountains. Here there are heavy forests where wild boar and goats, deer, lynx, and the rare European bison roam the rugged crags and valleys. The highest peak is Mount Rysy (*Ri-si*) in the Tatras.

Grains—rye, wheat, barley, oats, and others—make up over 60 percent of the total agricultural production. Potatoes, a staple of the Polish diet, are the next most important crop. Sugar beets, tobacco, flax for linen, and hemp for twine, are grown. Pig farming produces the famous Polish hams and sausages. Cattle and sheep are also raised. More than a quarter of the land is forested, mainly in pine and other evergreens that provide timber and wood pulp for Polish industry and for export.

Coal is Poland's "black gold." It is the basis of the steel and manufacturing industries that, since World War II, have replaced agriculture as the main source of the nation's wealth. The most extensive deposits are in Silesia, in the southwestern part of the country. Silesian coal is the basis for the great steel industry of this region. Although a little iron is mined just north of the coal region, most of the ore to feed the blast furnaces and steel mills of the Silesian industrial cities must be imported. Coal, burned to operate steam engines, provides most of the country's electricity. It is also the raw material for a growing chemical and synthetic fiber industry.

In the southern mining belt, lead, zinc, copper, and uranium, as well as some tin, manganese, and lignite are produced, although not in large enough quantity to make Poland self-sufficient. Salt, mined near Wieliczka (Vye-*leech*-kah) and Bochnia (*Bokh*-nyah),

These buildings on a cobbled square in Warsaw are reminders of the old city, most of which was destroyed in World War II.

and sulfur are raw materials for the chemical industries. Petroleum and natural gas are produced near Rzeszow (*Zhe*-shoof) and in other areas.

Like industrial centers everywhere, many of the cities of Poland are grimy and crowded. Warsaw, with more than one million inhabitants, is a major manufacturing city. Textiles and clothing, machine tools, electrical equipment, furniture, and precision instruments are among the principal products. Lódz (*Wooj*), 75 miles to the southwest, is the second largest city of Poland and a center of textile, clothing and food-processing industries. Historic Poznan (*Poz*-nahn-yah), the first Polish capital, is a trade center and railroad junction. Wroclaw (*Wrots*-waf; or Breslau) on the Oder, Katowice (Kaht-oh-*vee*-tse), at the center of a complex of industrial cities in the Silesian coal region, and Lublin, an ancient trade city southeast of Warsaw, are other major centers of manufacturing.

Kraków (*Krah*-kof), the most beautiful and perhaps the oldest city in Poland, has always been the pride of Polish culture. From the fourteenth century until Warsaw was made the capital at the end of the sixteenth century, the Polish kings ruled from their castle on Wawel Hill. Their tombs are in the cathedral

nearby. The university, where the great sixteenth-century astronomer Copernicus was a student has been a center of learning for 600 years. Today, Kraków is a busy commercial city.

Częstochowa (Ches-to-*kho*-vah), a manufacturing city in the iron mining region northeast of Kraków, is an old religious center.

Three good ports on the Baltic are the bases for Poland's growing maritime traffic and ship-building industry. Gdansk (Danzig) from earliest times was the leading port of the region, and was an independent city-state between the two world wars. Recently it has been surpassed by Gdynia (Gu-*dee*-nyah), a new city 12 miles to the north, founded in 1921. Coal ships load at Szczecin (*Shche*-tseen; or Stettin, Shte-*teen*) at the mouth of the Oder.

These ports handle Poland's exports and imports. Most of its foreign trade commerce is with other Communist countries, and with the United Kingdom, Germany, and the United States.

The Poles are a Slavic people who speak a language akin to Russian. They have a fierce national pride that has survived a long history of intervention and domination by more powerful neighbors. In the ninth century, their ancestors established a kingdom with its capital at Poznan. For hundreds of years the Polish plains were a battlefield as the small Slavic nation resisted the attacks of Germans, Swedes, Lithuanians, Bohemians, and Russians, and Mongol forays in the Middle Ages. Intermarriage with the royal families of Lithuania and Hungary in the fourteenth century created the Jagellonian dynasty, which at the height of Poland's "Golden Age" in the fifteenth and sixteenth centuries, ruled territory from the Baltic to the Black Sea.

Because they had been converted to Roman Catholicism early in their history, the Poles were often in conflict with the Greek Orthodox Slavs of Russia and had closer cultural ties with the West. They distinguished themselves as champions of Christianity in fighting the Moslem advance in Europe, most notably under King John Sobieski, who turned back the Turks at the decisive battle of Vienna in 1683.

The origins of Poland's decline rest with the Seym, a parliament of nobles that gradually gained power at the expense of the crown, leaving the country without strong leadership. In the seventeenth century Russia won part of the Ukraine and Sweden acquired a section of Pomerania. The fear of Russian domination of Poland decided Frederick the Great of Prussia and Empress Maria Theresa of Austria to join with Catherine the Great of Russia in dividing up the country. Large areas were annexed by these three rulers in 1772 and 1793, leaving only a small central section

independent. Following a rebellion led by the patriot Kosciusko (who also fought in the American Revolution) a final partition completed the division of Poland in 1795. The stubborn Poles rose up several times in the nineteenth century, but not until the defeat of Germany and the break-up of Austro-Hungarian Empire in World War I did Poland regain its independence and territory, including eastern lands won in a 1920 war with the Bolshevik government of Russia.

Between the wars Poland was under the near-dictatorship of Marshall Jozef Pilsudski and other military leaders. The Jews, Germans, Russians, and

Workers gather at the gate of iron-smelting works in Walbrzych, Poland. Modern Poland is becoming heavily industrialized.

Lithuanians who made up a third of the population, suffered harsh repression by the Poles. World War II began when Germany—having first secured the complicity of the Soviet Union through a nonaggression pact—demanded the return of the Free City of Danzig. Poland, backed up by an alliance with Great Britain and France, refused. Hitler's army invaded Poland on September 1, 1939. Seventeen days later Russian troops occupied the eastern half of the country, but lost it in 1941 when Germany attacked the USSR.

Some of the most brutal acts of the war took place in Poland. The Jews, who had a thousand-year-old community in Poland, were cold-bloodedly exterminated by the Germans. Some three million Jews were starved to death or executed in infamous concentration camps such as Auschwitz (*Oush*-vits; or Oswięcm, Osh-*vye*-cheem), and in Warsaw's walled ghetto. The Russians slaughtered 10,000 Polish officers in the Katyn Forest and buried them in a mass grave. Meanwhile, a Polish army in exile fought bravely with the Allied forces, and an underground movement harrassed the Germans in Poland.

The Soviet army liberated Poland in 1944-45 and after the War Russian influence enforced the establishment of a Communist régime. At the Potsdam Conference (1945) farm lands in the east comprising 46 per cent of pre-war Poland were ceded to the Soviet Union, while Danzig and German territory east of the Oder and Neisse rivers (with the exception of the old East Prussia on the Baltic, which was taken by Russia) reverted to Poland.

The Communist government has had trouble keeping the stubbornly independent Poles in line. Polish farmers sabotaged the effort to place all agriculture under state collective farms. Intellectuals, always a potent force in a country that has produced such giants as the composer Frederic Chopin, Nobel prize-winning physicist Marie Curie, pianist-statesman Ignac Jan Paderewski, and author Joseph Conrad, spoke out for more freedom of thought. Finally the industrial workers rebelled against their low standard of living in the Poznan riots of 1956. A more independent Communist leadership headed by Premier Wladyslaw Gomulka was installed. Today Poland has more contact with the United States and the West than any other Communist satellite nation.

Pictures of Marx and Lenin look over the crowd gathered for a May Day celebration in Red Square, Moscow.

SOVIET UNION

The largest country in the world is the Union of Soviet Socialist Republics, generally called the Soviet Union. It occupies one-sixth of the land area of the globe, sprawling across eastern Europe and northern Asia. Because of the great size of the Soviet Union and the more than one hundred different nationalities among its citizens, the country includes many widely differing geographic and cultural regions. Vast grasslands, called steppes, provide farm and grazing land across the central part of the country. North of the steppe are great forests and the cold, treeless land called tundra. To the south and east, along the borders with Afghanistan, China, and Mongolia, lie high mountains and deserts. The climate and scenery of the Black Sea coast is Mediterranean. In the Far East rise high plateaus and ice-capped mountains. More than three-fourths of the population of the Soviet Union is Slavic, and the Slavic Russians have dominated the country since the defeat of the Mongols in the late fifteenth century.

For centuries, the Russians led a rural, almost medieval existence under the despotic rule of the tsars. Change came violently with the revolution of 1917. Since then Russia—renamed officially the Union of Soviet Socialist Republics—has been governed by a Communist dictatorship. By strict government control of all aspects of the life and work of the people, and at the cost of suppressing personal freedom and comforts, the Communists have developed their natural resources and transformed the country from a backward agricultural land into a mighty industrial empire.

Mountains rise from the plains of Kazakstan near Alma-Ata in Soviet Central Asia.

SOVIET UNION
⊛ Capital

Moscow..............D 6

Physical Features

EASTERN SOVIET UNION
Principal Cities
Pop.—Thousands

Lambert Azimuthal Equal Area Projection
SCALE 1:28,000,000   1 Inch = 442 Statute Miles

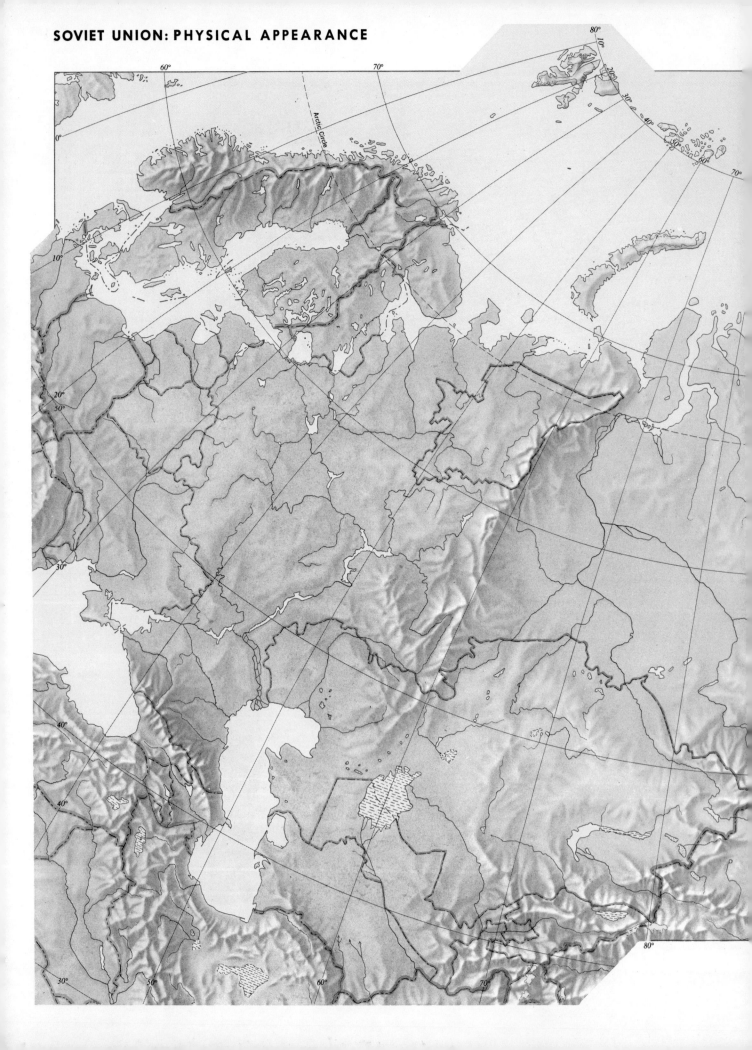

163

The map represents
land elevation
by showing
the landscape
strongly lighted
from the northwest.
Highlights and
shadows define the
mountains and hills.

Arctic Circle

70°

80°

160°

130°

140°

130°

120°

110°

100°

180°

60°

170°

160°

50°

150°

140°

40°

130°

120°

110°

100°

SOVIET UNION

▲ SEE MAP PAGES 160–161, 168–169, 170–171

Capital: Moscow

Population (1962): 220,000,000
  Density: 26 per square mile
  Distribution: Urban: 40 per cent
    Rural: 60 per cent

Area: 8,599,300 square miles

Elevation: Highest point: 24,590 feet
  Lowest point: 433 feet below sea level

Principal language: Russian

Principal religion: Orthodox

Political divisions: 15 republics

Currency unit: Rouble

National holidays: November 7, 8 Anniversary of the "October Revolution"

National anthem: *Gimn sovetskovo soyuza* (The opening line, translated, reads: "Indestructible union of free republics")

Man made his first orbit of the earth in the Vostok I, a Russian spacecraft.

Vendors sell flowers, balloons, and food on a Moscow street. In the right background is a newsstand.

As the first Soviet cosmonaut circled the earth at 17,000 miles per hour, he spent twenty minutes over his own country, the vast territory of the Union of Soviet Socialist Republics. At its farthest points the Soviet Union measures 6,000 miles from west to east and 3,000 miles from north to south.

Had he been able to see the whole of the Soviet Union at one time, the cosmonaut would have observed patterns of colors that mark the different regions of the country. A triangular area of green, with a broad base at the borders of eastern Europe and an apex pointed at the highlands of Central Asia, reaches halfway across the center of the land. This is called the western forest region because it was once covered with broad-leaf trees. It is now the best farm land in the Soviet Union. Just south of it is the steppe, level grassland given over to farming and grazing. To the north, areas of darker green indicate the dense Russian and Siberian coniferous forests. Still farther north the gray-brown of the tundra appears, land with permanently frozen subsoil. South of the steppes in Asia, a zone of brown marks dry plains and deserts. Beyond the plains, the eastern half of the country rises in barren highlands and snow-capped mountains.

Most of the highlands fringe the borders of the Soviet Union. The low Urals are an exception. Extending southward from the Arctic coast, they divide the wide plains. With the Ural River, which empties into the Caspian Sea, they form the traditional dividing line between Europe and Asia. The Carpathians cross the western corner of the Great Russian Plain at the borders of Romania, Hungary, Czechoslovakia, and Poland. The Caucasus Mountains lie between the Black Sea and the Caspian, near the borders of Turkey and Iran. The mountains rise higher still in Asia. A broad band of lofty mountains and high plateaus begins along the southern border and reaches all the way to Bering Strait.

Many rivers drain this immense country. The

UNION OF SOVIET SOCIALIST REPUBLICS
ECONOMY

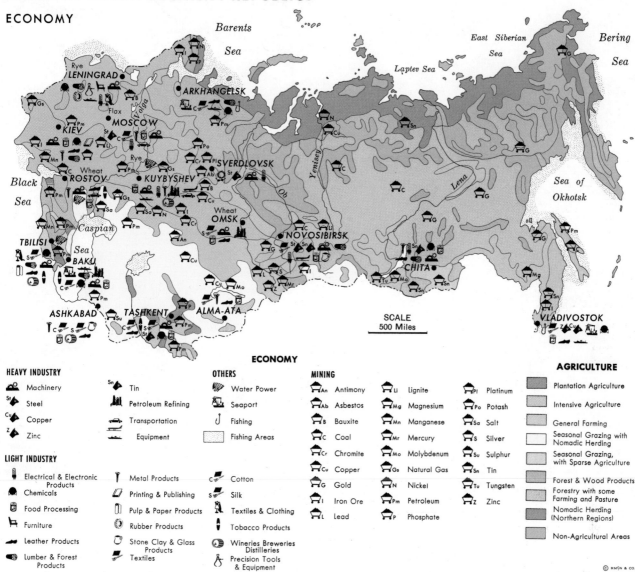

ECONOMY

HEAVY INDUSTRY
- Machinery
- Sn Tin
- St Steel
- Cu Copper
- Z Zinc

LIGHT INDUSTRY
- Electrical & Electronic Products
- Chemicals
- Food Processing
- Furniture
- Leather Products
- Lumber & Forest Products

- Petroleum Refining
- Transportation
- Equipment
- Metal Products
- Printing & Publishing
- Pulp & Paper Products
- Rubber Products
- Stone Clay & Glass Products
- Textiles

OTHERS
- Water Power
- Seaport
- Fishing
- Fishing Areas
- C Cotton
- S Silk
- Textiles & Clothing
- Tobacco Products
- Wineries Breweries Distilleries
- Precision Tools & Equipment

MINING
- An Antimony
- Ab Asbestos
- B Bauxite
- C Coal
- Cr Chromite
- Cu Copper
- G Gold
- I Iron Ore
- L Lead
- Li Lignite
- Mg Magnesium
- Mn Manganese
- Mr Mercury
- Mo Molybdenum
- Gs Natural Gas
- N Nickel
- Pm Petroleum
- P Phosphate
- Pl Platinum
- Po Potash
- Sa Salt
- S Silver
- Su Sulphur
- Sn Tin
- Tu Tungsten
- Z Zinc

AGRICULTURE
- Plantation Agriculture
- Intensive Agriculture
- General Farming
- Seasonal Grazing with Nomadic Herding
- Seasonal Grazing, with Sparse Agriculture
- Forest & Wood Products
- Forestry with some Farming and Pasture
- Nomadic Herding (Northern Regions)
- Non-Agricultural Areas

© RMcN & CO.

Volga, Europe's longest river, winds 2,290 miles from northwest of Moscow to the Caspian Sea. The Dnestr (Dun-*ye*-stur; or Dniester), Dnepr (Dun-*ye*-pur; or Dnieper, *Nee*-pur), and Don rivers cross the Ukraine to empty into the Black Sea. The dams at Zaporozhye (Zu-per-*oh*-zha-ye) on the Dnepr and at Volgograd on the Volga furnish power for two of the largest hydroelectric stations in the world. The great rivers of Siberia—as Soviet Asia is called—are the Ob (*Ohb*), which crosses the West Siberian Lowland, the Yenisey (Ye-ne-*say*), which divides the plain from the Central Siberian Uplands, the 2,650-mile Lena (*Lay*-nah), longest in the Soviet Union, and the Amur (Ah-*moor*), which forms the boundary with China.

Temperatures grow more severe from west to east.

Summers are hot, winters are cold, and rainfall is relatively light over most of the country. In Siberia, the temperatures are extreme; the annual highs range from around 120 degrees at the Afghanistan border to 32 degrees on the arctic coast. Northeastern Siberia is the coldest inhabited region on earth. In the west of the European section of the Soviet Union as much as 30 to 40 inches of rain may fall in a year, with 60 inches in the Caucasus Mountains. East of the Urals rain diminishes, and an annual rainfall of less than 2 inches is normal in the Central Asian deserts.

The Soviet Union is popularly called Russia because the Slavic Russian people, numbering more than half the population, have historically dominated the country. Two other Slavic peoples, the Ukranians of

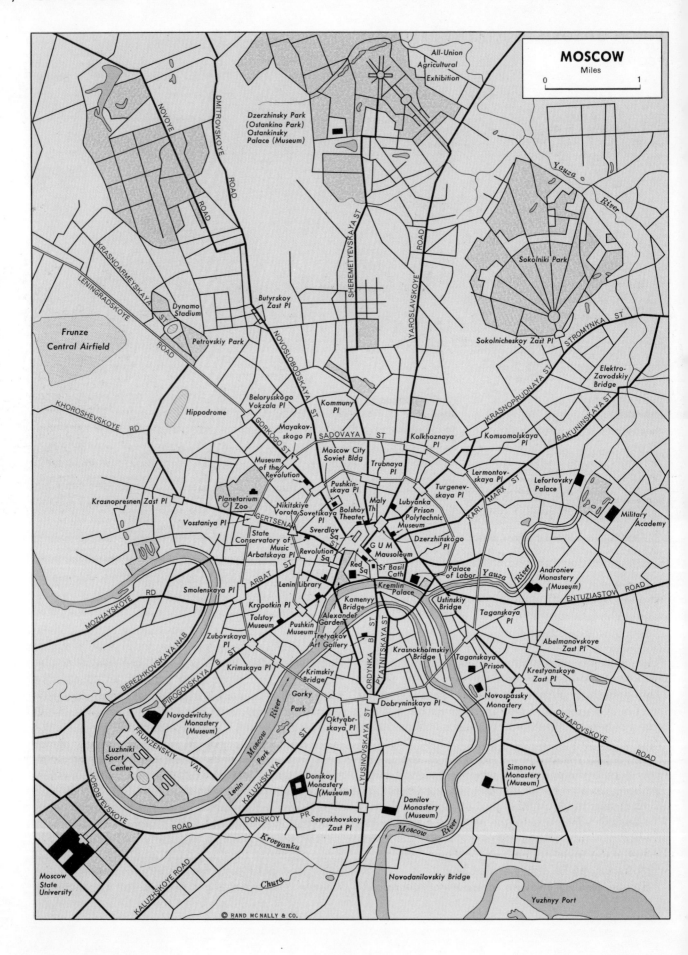

MOSCOW
Miles
0   1

In Red Square, Moscow, people wait in a long line to enter the Mausoleum, where Lenin's body still rests.

southern Europe and the Byelorussians (White Russians), with other smaller groups, Polish, and Lithuanians, make up a Slavic population that is three-fourths the national total. More than one hundred distinct nationalities speak their own languages, but use Russian as a second tongue.

In the great tribal migrations of ancient and medieval times many peoples from Asia swept across what is now the Soviet Union. Their descendants are identified today by their languages. The Finno-Ugric peoples, who have linguistic ties with the people of Finland and Hungary, are found in European USSR. The Baltic language area includes the Lithuanians and Latvians. The Moldavians, along the border with Romania, speak a language with Latin roots. The Caucasus contains several language families, including Georgian, Armenian, Kurdish, and Turkic peoples. In the Far East of Siberia live Mongol, Samoyed, and Tungus-Manchu peoples, formerly nomadic Asiatic tribesmen who are now becoming farmers.

For political purposes, all these peoples are grouped in fifteen Soviet Socialist Republics, generally called Union Republics. These are further subdivided, with all units based on nationalities within the Soviet Union. In a class by itself is the Russian Soviet Federal Socialist Republic. It includes three-fourths of the country's area and more than half of its population. It encompasses the central and northern portions of the European USSR and Siberia. The Ukrainian Soviet Socialist Republic occupies most of the south European portion of the Soviet Union and is second in population. Each Union Republic is theoretically entitled to have its own government and to maintain foreign relations independently. The Ukrainian and Byelorussian republics, in fact, are charter members of the United Nations, along with the Soviet Union itself.

The urban heart of Russia is Moscow, with a population of more than 8,000,000. At its center is a walled city, the Kremlin. Once the Kremlin housed the tsars.

WESTERN SOVIET UNION

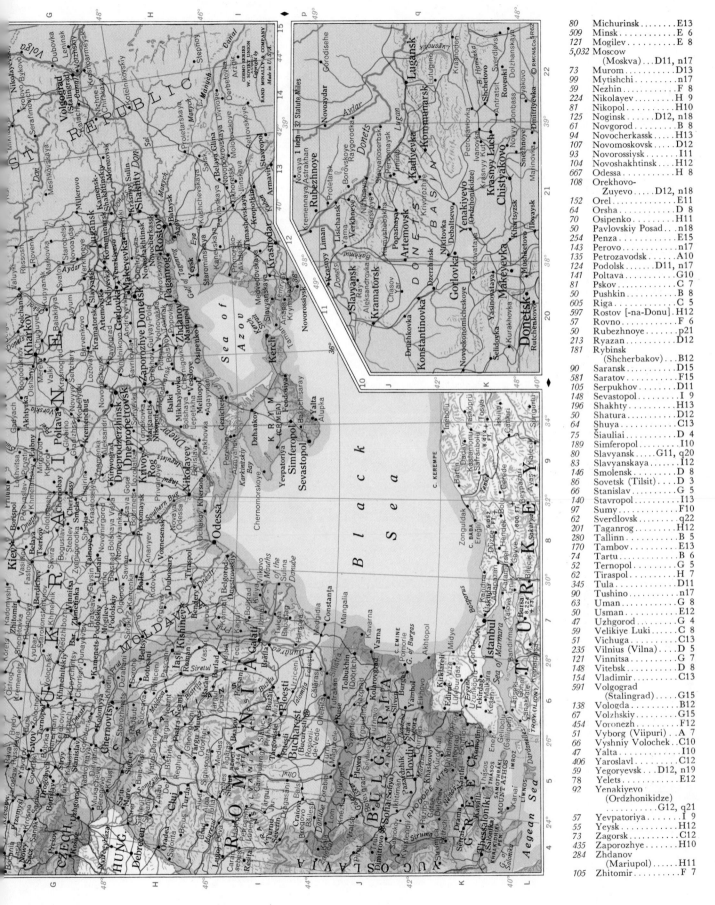

Conic Projection

SCALE 1:8,000,000   1 Inch = 126 Statute Miles

SOUTH CENTRAL SOVIET UNION

Sinusoidal Projection
SCALE 1: 11,400,000   1 Inch = 180 Statute Miles

Women at work on a cooperative farm in the Ukraine. This land is part of the level steppe, or grassland, of the Soviet Union.

Melons in a market in Samarkand. This city is in the desert region of Central Asia, and farming depends upon irrigation.

Today, the palaces are government buildings and museums. Nearby is Red Square, with the onion-domed St. Basil's Church at one end and the tomb of Lenin, the father of the Russian Revolution, in the center. The Moscow University building is a modern skyscraper. The Moscow subway is famous for its efficiency, its extent—there are forty miles of track—and the elegance of its stations.

On the Gulf of Finland, Leningrad, founded as St. Petersburg by Czar Peter the Great in 1703, is the cultural capital of the Soviet Union. It is also the most important port and a manufacturing center. Kiev (*Kee*-ef), the capital of the Ukrainian SSR, has modern buildings in the box-like Soviet style, as well as churches dating from the Middle Ages. Odessa is the main Black Sea port. The smoke of heavy industry hangs over Gorkiy (*Gor*-kee), 260 miles east of Moscow, and over Kharkov (*Kar*-kof), 400 miles to the south. Other large industrial cities are Sverdlovsk (*Sverd*-lofsk), and Chelyabinsk (Chil-*yah*-binsk). Baku (Bah-*koo*), on the Caspian, is the center for the Soviet Union's most productive oil region. In Asia, the fascinating mosques and bazaars of Tashkent, Samarkand, and Bukhara stand beside modern government buildings. Novosibirsk (Nuh-vuh-see-*beersk*) is sometimes called "the Chicago of Siberia." It bustles with the

Arctic Ocean

WESTERN

FOREST

SOUTHERN FOREST

Dvina

N. Dvina

Ob

Yenisey

Lena

Amur

Sea of Okhotsk

Lake Baikal

ARCTIC CIRCLE

Dnepr

Don

Volga

Ural

Caspian Sea

Aral Sea

Syr Darya

Amu Darya

Lake Balkhash

500 MILES

Taiga (Cone-bearing forest)	Steppe
Forest (Broad-leaved and mixed forest)	Tundra
Glacier	Desert

NATURAL VEGETATION OF THE SOVIET UNION

activity of people building on a new frontier. Vladi-vostok (*Vlah*-de-voh-stock) is Russia's principal Pacific port. In the USSR, there are some 150 cities with more than 100,000 population.

On the national level, government is in the hands of the Supreme Soviet of the USSR. The Supreme Soviet meets twice a year. It does not draft laws or make policy, but approves the decrees presented to it by the Council of Ministers. The Council of Ministers and the thirty-three-member Presidium of the Supreme Soviet run the country. They are chosen by the Supreme Soviet. The Chairman of the Presidium is the chief of state, but his duties are largely ceremonial. The real ruler of the USSR is the Chairman of the Council of Ministers, or Prime Minister, who is usually also Secretary of the Communist Party. The man who holds these offices—since 1954 it has been Nikita S. Khrushchev—has the powers of a dictator.

The Communist Party not only controls the national and local government, but it also influences the lives of every Soviet citizen through control of newspapers, schools, factories, farms, and community organizations from tiny villages to the wards of big cities. Policy decisions of the Party's Central Committee and the Political Bureau (Politburo) are passed on through nearly 500,000 Party branches called cells. The Party is thus a government within the government. There are fewer than 8,000,000 Party members in the USSR, but they occupy most of the positions of authority.

Russia has a heritage of oriental despotism and suspicion of foreigners. It remained feudal and isolated until comparatively recent times.

In the ninth century A.D., a viking chief named Rurik proclaimed himself ruler of a number of Slavic tribes in northern Europe and founded the original Russian state at Novgorod, about one hundred miles south of present-day Leningrad. Rurik's successor moved the capital south to Kiev, fought the Turkic Khazars, and united the Eastern Slavs. For three hun-

The GUM department store in Moscow is one of the show places of the Soviet Union.

The women pictured above are selling potatoes in a Moscow market. Potatoes are raised throughout the plains surrounding the city.

Caspian Sea fishermen have just caught a huge sturgeon. Sturgeon eggs are the caviar that brings a high price in world markets.

A textile mill in Taskent, a new industrial region of Central Asia. The manufacture of cloth is carried on in many Soviet regions.

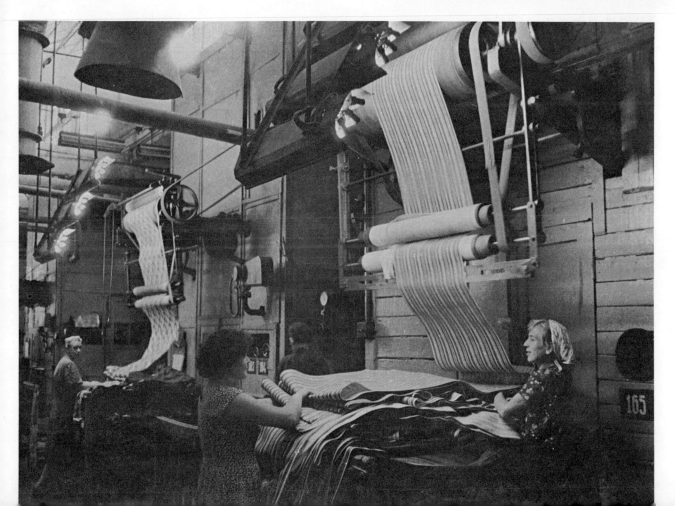

People of the Soviet Union are of many different backgrounds. These are Moslems at prayer in Central Asia.

dred years the duchy of Kiev was the most powerful Slavic state. It extended its control over the lower Volga region and part of the Caucasus and, in places, into the Balkans. In the tenth century the Kiev rulers adopted the Greek Orthodox form of Christianity and established cultural and commercial ties with the Byzantine Empire at Constantinople, seat of the religion's heirarchy. The Greek-derived Cyrillic alphabet, still used in Russia and the Balkans, grew from this contact.

In 1054 the Kiev duchy was divided into numerous feudal states. The Mongols descended on them in 1240, and for the next two hundred years held sway over most of European Russia and Central Asia. Then, in the fourteenth century, Moscow became the most powerful of the feudal states in eastern Russia until in 1480 it stopped paying tribute to the Mongols.

Ivan the Terrible (1533-1584) was the first grand duke of Moscow to take the title of tsar. His cossacks conquered the Mongols in Europe and most of Siberia. They became the world's most feared soldiers. By the seventeenth century they had carried the conquest of Siberia to the shores of the Pacific.

The most important and colorful of the tsars was Peter the Great (1689-1725). He founded a new capital on the Baltic—St. Petersburg (Leningrad)—as a symbol of his determination to modernize medieval Russia. He built the first Russian navy and fought to gain ice-free ports on the Black Sea and the Baltic so that Russia could become a maritime trading nation. The urge for "warm water windows" on the world has been a tenet of Russian foreign policy ever since.

Catherine the Great (1762-1796) added the Crimea and a large part of Poland to the empire. Alaska was colonized by Russian fur traders during her reign. She was a patron of art and science and a promoter of industry.

Russia was often at war in the nineteenth century. Napoleon's invasion was turned back in 1812. All of Poland and Finland, and Bessarabia (part of eastern Romania) were annexed. A bloody but inconclusive

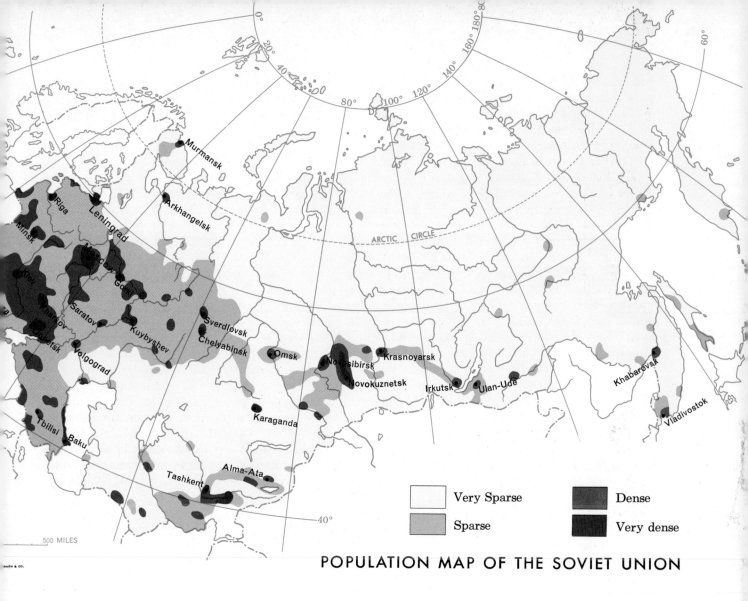

Very Sparse

Sparse

Dense

Very dense

500 MILES

war was fought against England, France, and Turkey in the Crimea. While Russia, in alliance with Austria, helped suppress revolutionary movements in Europe, the tsars continued their expansion in Asia. The independent areas of Turkestan between the Caspian and China were annexed. Central Asia was subdued. After territory up to the Manchurian border was acquired from China, Russian colonization of the Far East was intensified. Russia sold Alaska to the United States in 1867 for $7,200,000. Russia's last imperial adventure in the Far East, its attempt to annex Manchuria and Korea, led to the Russo-Japanese War of 1904-1905. The Russian defeat, added to domestic unrest, was to explode in revolution.

Ivan the Terrible had checked the power of the landholding nobles (boyars), but later tsars granted them extensive privileges in exchange for their support. Thus began serfdom, the servitude of peasants to landowners. By the mid-eighteenth century, millions of serfs were in fact slaves. Alexander II freed them in 1861, but it brought them little relief. City

dwellers, laboring in the factories that grew rapidly in the late nineteenth century also lived in great poverty, with no political rights. Discontent was rising among national and religious minorities persecuted by the harsh tsars. In some of the world's greatest literature, writers such as Tolstoi, Dostoevski, Gogol, Chekhov, and Gorki movingly portrayed the plight of the workers and peasants and the tensions building up within the corrupt empire. Intellectuals and students joined them in a call for reform.

On January 22, 1905, soldiers fired on a crowd marching with a petition to the tsar's winter palace in St. Petersburg. This spark ignited a series of strikes, riots, and mutinies. The government agreed to establish Russia's first parliament, the Duma, and to distribute lands to the peasants. The reforms were too little and too late. When Russia entered the war against Germany and the Austro-Hungarian Empire in 1914, the country was on the verge of chaos. In March, 1917, military defeats, food shortages, and continuing revolutionary agitation forced the abdication of Emperor Nicholas II. The provisional government that followed was overthrown in November by the radical Bolsheviks. The world's first national government based on the communist ideology of Karl Marx was established, with the Bolshevik leader, V. I. Lenin as virtual dictator.

For three years Lenin was engaged in a civil war waged by the opponents of Communism, a war with attacks by Poland, and in fighting off invasions by Allied troops. By 1922, when the Union of Soviet Socialist Republics was established, the former empire had shrunk. Russia had lost Finland, Estonia, Latvia, Lithuania, its Polish territories, and Bessarabia. After Lenin's death in 1924, power was held briefly by Leon Trotsky. He was opposed by many Communist Party leaders and was banished from the country in 1929. Even before this, the dictatorship was seized by Josef V. Stalin who ruled until he died in 1953.

After World War II, the Soviet Union annexed the three Baltic states, East Prussia, parts of Poland and Finland (which the Soviet Union fought in a brief war in 1939-1940, and continued to fight after entering the war against Germany in 1941), an area in Romania, a section in the Carpathians, ceded by Czechoslovakia, and the Sakhalin and Kurile islands surrendered by Japan. At least six million Russians were killed and fourteen million wounded in the war. Despite heavy losses and widespread destruction, the

Soviet Union emerged from the war a super-power. East Germany and the Central European and Balkan countries liberated from the Nazis fell under its control.

The most impressive achievement of the Communist regime, however, is the transformation of the Soviet Union from a backward agricultural nation to a giant industrial power in which all the means of production are owned by the state. The Soviet Union claims to have increased industrial production to more than thirty-six times that of pre-World War I levels.

The country is virtually self-sufficient in raw materials. The Soviet Union is the world's leading producer of coal, iron ore, manganese, and timber. It ranks second in production of cement, chrome, gold, lead, steel, zinc ore, and electricity. It is third in petroleum and aluminum. Huge deposits of salt and potash help form the base of a huge chemical industry.

The Donets Basin in the Ukraine and Kuznets Basin in Siberia are rich in coal. Iron is found in the Ukraine, the Urals, and Siberia. Baku, in the Caucasus, was the main pre-war oil center, but larger deposits have since been found in Eastern European Russia, Central Asia, Kazakhstan (Kah-zakh-*stan*), and the Far East. With the development of new resources, heavy industry is moving from the Moscow-Leningrad area into the Ukraine, the Urals, and Siberia.

In agriculture, production gains have also been spectacular, although the inefficiency of the state collective farms required a major overhaul of the system after Stalin's death. Russia is the world's top producer of wheat, sugar, and potatoes, and is second or third in barley, butter, cotton, meat, milk, oats, and wool. Grains, sugar beets, and livestock are raised in the Ukraine and on the steppes on both sides of the Urals. Cotton is planted in Central Asia. New "virgin lands" in Siberia are now being brought into cultivation.

Prewar exports were Russian timber products, grain, furs, caviar from the Caspian, and petroleum; imports were machinery and equipment, metals, rubber, and textiles. Today, Russia exports machinery and metals and more oil, but the traditional products are no longer so important. The country now imports far less machinery and finished metals, but more special ores and consumer goods. Most of the trade is with the satellite nations and China.

The rapid development forced on the Soviet people in the past forty-five years has emphasized heavy industry at the expense of consumer goods. Although Khrushchev has promised more food, better housing, and comforts for the Russians, their standard of living is still well below that of the West.

Nothing has dramatized the new power of the Soviet Union better than its achievements in science and technology.

Leningrad's completely modern dock facilities have made the city the Soviet Union's leading port for international trade.

A barge hauling logs past Moscow on the Moscow River. One of the city's skyscrapers towers in the background.

INDEX OF COUNTRIES

Copyright by
RAND McNALLY & COMPANY
Made in U.S.A.

Longitude East of Greenwich